CW00431314

VALUING MONEY

Text copyright © Chris Hudson 2015

Illustrations copyright © Simon Smith 2015

The author asserts the moral right to be identified as the author of this work

Published by
The Bible Reading Fellowship
15 The Chambers, Vineyard
Abingdon OX14 3FE
United Kingdom
Tel: +44 (0)1865 319700
Email: enquiries@brf.org.uk
Website: www.brf.org.uk
BRF is a Registered Charity

ISBN 978 0 85746 121 6

First published 2015
10 9 8 7 6 5 4 3 2 1 0
All rights reserved

Acknowledgements

Unless otherwise stated, scripture quotations are taken from the Contemporary English Version of the Bible published by HarperCollins Publishers, copyright © 1991, 1992, 1995 American Bible Society.

Scripture quotations taken from the Holy Bible, English Standard Version, published by HarperCollins Publishers, © 2001 Crossway Bibles, a division of Good News Publishers. Used by permission. All rights reserved.

Scripture quotations taken from The Holy Bible, New International Version (Anglicised edition) copyright © 1979, 1984, 2011 by Biblica. Used by permission of Hodder & Stoughton Publishers, an Hachette UK company. All rights reserved. 'NIV' is a registered trademark of Biblica. UK trademark number 1448790.

Cover photos: Thinkstock: © Mike Rickword © Joe Gough • Shutterstock: © Katy Spichal • iStock: © Bluestocking © Rouzes

Every effort has been made to trace and contact copyright owners for material used in this resource. We apologise for any inadvertent omissions or errors, and would ask those concerned to contact us so that full acknowledgement can be made in the future.

A catalogue record for this book is available from the British Library

Printed by Gutenberg Press, Tarxien, Malta

VALUING
MONEY

A 10-UNIT RE PROGRAMME HELPING CHILDREN UNPACK THE REAL VALUE OF MONEY

CHRIS HUDSON

Important information
Photocopying permission

The right to photocopy material in *Valuing Money* is granted for the pages that contain the photocopying clause: 'Reproduced with permission from *Valuing Money* by Chris Hudson (Barnabas in Schools, 2015)' so long as reproduction is for use in a teaching situation by the original purchaser. The right to photocopy material is not granted for anyone other than the original purchaser without written permission from BRF.

The Copyright Licensing Agency (CLA)

If you are resident in the UK and you have a photocopying licence with the Copyright Licensing Agency (CLA) please check the terms of your licence. If your photocopying request falls within the terms of your licence, you may proceed without seeking further permission. If your request exceeds the terms of your CLA licence, please contact the CLA directly with your request. Copyright Licensing Agency, Saffron House, 6–10 Kirby Street, London EC1N 8TS. Telephone 020 7400 3100; fax 020 7400 3101; email cla@cla.co.uk; website www.cla.co.uk. The CLA will provide photocopying authorisation and royalty fee information on behalf of BRF.

BRF is a Registered Charity (No. 233280)

Contents

Making the most of this book

How is this topic relevant to our pupils?

You can tell what God thinks of money by the type of people he gives most of it to. ANON

Money doesn't really exist. Think about it for a moment. That credit card is just a piece of plastic. Those coins or notes are just pieces of metal or paper, collectively assigned a 'value' that measures its actual worth to us at any given place and time. The bar of chocolate we buy might cost us 65p at the shop around the corner, because the shopkeeper assumes she can get us to pay that sum. If we take the trouble to drive to the out-of-town supermarket, the price might be lower (although we'll probably be spending money on other things too while we're there).

Furthermore, we have all agreed (in the United Kingdom, at least) to pay for our chocolate bars in pounds and pence. In the Republic of Ireland we would pay for them in euros and cents, and, in the USA, we'd use dollars and cents. Let's explore the 'value' of that chocolate bar further. The 65 pence that we spend may be a small proportion of our personal income. If we are in paid employment, our income was paid to us as a measurement of what our employer (or customer) thought our labour was worth. They could have paid us in sea shells or kisses, but that would be awkward and unhygienic—and it might turn some people into millionaires quite quickly! So money is just a shared symbol for use in transactions, a kind of social contract that works only by mutual agreement. We could replace our 'currency' with community credits or bartered goods or services, but someone, somewhere, still has to decide how we measure and compare the 'worth' or 'value' of different goods and services, and everyone else has to agree with that decision.

Once we start using money for transactions, it can also become a measure of our personal status, influence and prestige, or our lack of them. Money can buy property, comfort and security, including the assurance of food on the table tomorrow and next week. It can also buy freedom from want, hardship and the need to rely on others. (One newspaper supplement on personal finance was headed 'Take control of your life'.) Equally, money can be used generously to feed the hungry and support the weak or to endow the creation of artworks and music that lift the soul and spirit. So, we have to learn to be responsible with it.

Every child understands that money is a useful tool for getting us the things we want, but it takes time to understand that there's more to personal finance than simply getting cash from a hole in the wall and spending it. In the same way that maintaining a healthy body requires an understanding of nutrition, the maintenance of healthy personal finance requires a grasp of cash flow, noting how money moves into a bank account and out again. Children need to understand that money doesn't just 'happen': somebody, somewhere, has to earn it in some way before we can spend it, or we fall into debt—which is why having a regular part-time job is an excellent way for a child to learn financial independence from a young age. We also have to understand the difference between 'wants' and 'needs': we cannot (and should not) ever expect to be able to buy everything we desire, despite the best efforts of the advertisers.

Why teach about money in Religious Education?

There are some excellent initiatives encouraging primary schools to take money education seriously, but few explore the moral or spiritual dimensions. Religious Education can play a powerful role in connecting and extending a school's offering of Spiritual, Moral, Social and Cultural education, because RE is about examining and extending a child's understanding of values. So, any RE topic exploring 'the difference that faith makes to life' should involve some discussion of the way money is understood and used. Interestingly, according to the Christian Bible, Jesus Christ had a great deal more to say about avarice (lust for money) than he ever did about sexual issues, likening it to the worship of other gods (Matthew 6:19–21, 24).

Valuing Money uses Religious Education to connect the SMSC part of the broader primary school curriculum with Numeracy, supporting the following generic RE topics. (Thanks to Lisa Fenton of Blackburn Diocese for this list.)

Rules for life

- What are rules?
- Why do we have rules?
- Who makes the rules?
- Is there a difference between rules and laws?
- What would happen if there were no rules?

Change the world

- What matters most to me?
- If you could change the world, what would you change? Why?
- Can I make a difference? How can I make a difference?
- How could you change the world?

What matters most?

- How do you decide what matters most?
- Who helps you decide what matters most?
- What are the key elements of friendship?
- What does God tell us matters most?

Harvest

- Why do we celebrate harvest festival?
- Where does our food come from?
- Which foods do you enjoy the most?
- How can we help those who do not have a good harvest?
- Why should we help those who do not have a good harvest?

People of faith

- What is faith?
- What does it mean for a person to have faith?
- What does it mean to be a person of faith?
- What motivates people of faith?
- How does having faith affect people's lives?

Wisdom

- What is a proverb?
- What is the message of the proverb we are studying today?
- Is this proverb still relevant today?
- What is wisdom? Who gives us wisdom?
- Who is wise?

Of course, RE is taught across the country through a variety of locally determined syllabuses, but we hope that the materials provided here are adaptable enough to suit the needs of your own school.

Applying the values

Values matter and, if we don't discuss them with children when discussing money, then the children lose out. Our values shape our attitudes and choices, whether we are saving, spending or giving money away. But isn't maths morally neutral? Not if we start applying the mathematics of money to everyday life, because immediately we face moral and spiritual questions. Children understand this very quickly as soon as they start acquiring pocket money.

- How do I get more pocket money? (Is it just about getting older? Do I need to earn it? Is pocket money a reward for being good? Can I supplement it by doing odd jobs or a paper round, or will that mean the pocket money stops? Can I sell unwanted toys or games?)
- How do I spend my pocket money? (Is money just there to make my life as pleasant and comfortable as possible? Can I spend it on absolutely anything I want? Is it worth saving up for something special? Can I make money from saving?)
- Why do others get more (or less) pocket money than I do? (Is that fair? What does fairness mean, anyway? Is there a right amount of pocket money for all children or should we just accept that each family does things its own way?)
- Should I borrow money from my friends or lend it to others? (Why do it? What could go right—or wrong?)

And here's a bonus question: why is stealing from Mum's purse wrong?

Of course, these child-sized questions all naturally extend into their adult equivalents, which is why financial education is so important. Financial education also shows up the values we're using and teaching. For example, most money 'problems' in maths schemes involve spending cash, but very few involve giving it away. Most charitable efforts in school involve making one-off contributions to a cause, but any charity will tell you that they much prefer being given regular tax-efficient payments over a given term. (Which do we prefer doing, and why?) Many fundraising efforts, such as the National Lottery, offer prizes in raffles or sweepstakes, promising the chance of winning a substantial prize, but few ask individuals simply to make a generous donation for a worthy cause.

Discussion of attitudes and values needs to go much deeper than encouraging pupils to 'make an informed choice'. Otherwise, we shouldn't be surprised if our children interpret that phrase to mean, 'You can do whatever you like if you think about it first.' The history of faith and belief includes discussions of work ethics, pride, avarice, fraud, speculation and greed, questions about the long-term consequences of selfishness and materialism, and demands for the rich to take responsibility for the care of the poor. Our children need tools like these to question the assumptions of our money culture, to navigate it safely in future and, especially, to wonder more about what it means to be thankful and generous.

How should we use this book?

Each unit in this book includes a story, RE material, cross-curricular content related to Literacy, Numeracy and other subject areas, and a script for circle time/classroom assembly. There is also an appendix of further ideas for giving an ethical dimension to Numeracy investigations and problems relating to money.

The stories in this book are listed below, with an indication of the RE topics for which they are suitable. All of them are suitable for work relating to Sacred texts/The Christian Bible/What Christians believe.

- Unit 1: The million-dollar note
  What matters most / Wisdom / People of faith / Harvest

- Unit 2: Isaac Newton, currency detective
  Rules for life / What matters most? / Wisdom

- Unit 3: The Emperor of the Earth Dragon
  Harvest / Change the world / People of faith / What matters most? / Wisdom

- Unit 4: A penny for your thoughts
  Rules for life / Change the world / People of faith / What matters most?

- Unit 5: It's not fair!
  Rules for life / Harvest / Change the world / People of faith / What matters most?

- Unit 6: So why do you want this job?
  Rules for life / Change the world / What matters most? / Wisdom

- Unit 7: Tulips from Amsterdam
  Rules for life / Change the world / What matters most? / Wisdom

- Unit 8: Wings on his feet
  Change the world / People of faith / What matters most?

- Unit 9: Bittersweet
  Rules for life / Harvest / Change the world / People of faith / What matters most? / Wisdom

- Unit 10: Visiting time
  Rules for life / Harvest / Change the world / What matters most?

Using the Christian Bible in primary school

The extracts in this resource are taken from the Contemporary English Version of the Bible. Biblical texts provide excellent stimulus for discussion and response, but they need to be carefully chosen and rendered in appropriate child-friendly language. There is a wealth of good translations and paraphrased versions available on the market, including *The Barnabas Schools Bible* (Barnabas for Schools, 2012) and the Children's International Version (UK). Downloads of Bible texts in a range of modern translations can also be found at www.biblegateway.com. For further ideas about handling Bible stories in school, see our website: www.barnabasinschools.org.uk.

Using drama and storytelling in RE

Acting and role play are an important part of many of the activities included in this book because they are inclusive, allowing pupils of all abilities to participate in the stories and experience them through the imagination. This approach allows pupils to grasp the human dilemmas in the stories for themselves and then reflect on whether or not they would respond in the same way as the characters did. Teaching RE like this isn't easier, but it can be a lot more fun, provided that pupils are given clear expectations about behaviour and respecting others in discussion. Schools workers and teachers have often found that techniques like these are highly successful at engaging pupils who have apparently 'switched off' from RE.

A good dramatised RE session will include warm-up games to introduce key vocabulary and ideas, clear organisation of pupil groups and opportunities for discussion. The use of 'talking partners' always speeds up preparations for speaking and listening. Discussion also gets more interesting when pupils are encouraged to generate questions about the story instead of simply answering questions set by the teacher. Written responses can be included, but a higher quality of responses is preferable to a greater quantity. Sometimes, allowing pupils to illustrate their ideas quickly as cartoons or diagrams will generate richer responses, provided that the efforts are clearly labelled and explained. If your classroom has space for drama and deskwork, experiment by alternating short drama sessions with fast written responses, to get thoughts down on paper immediately.

Stories and lesson material

Unit 1

What is money?

Background for teachers

Money increases the variety of ways in which people can make a living, by making it easier to exchange goods and services for a recognised rate. The poultry farmer who needs a roof repair doesn't have to pay the local builder in eggs or chickens because she can use money, and the builder isn't left with a load of eggs and chickens that he can't use. But using money can lead to problems, too. Wages and prices can rise and fall, affecting the amount of cash everybody has available for personal spending or saving.

The idea of using money as currency started spreading across the civilised world from around 400BC. For the first time in recorded history, units of exchange such as coins didn't need to be worth their weight in precious refined metal such as gold, silver, copper or bronze. Instead, they were worth what the authorities said they were worth. Having a shared currency made it easier to buy and sell within an agreed trading area, provided that everybody played by the same rules and the rate of exchange stayed fairly constant. If the situation changed (for example, if more silver coins came into circulation when a new silver mine opened), then the rates of exchange would alter, too.

However, some values might not be as reliable as we think. The rates of exchange can become unstable because of factors such as lower or higher productivity, famine, unrest, war or mass unemployment. Weird things happen, such as banknotes becoming literally not worth the paper they're printed on. This happened in Germany in the 1930s, but also in Zimbabwe in 2008, where the story in this unit is set. In Zimbabwe today, only relatively stable foreign currencies, such as the euro, South African rand or US dollars, are accepted and used in everyday life.

Story: The million-dollar note

Before telling this story, which is set in Zimbabwe, explain to your pupils that there's something a bit strange going on with the money. Can they spot it?

Femi was feeling hopeful that morning, as she pulled her cart along the dusty street. Her small loaves were well turned out, looking especially tasty, and the market-day weather was looking fine. There would be a good crowd. She'd been up before first light, mixing and baking and turning out loaf after loaf on her kitchen table. Now she only had to sell them at a good profit. It had cost her several million Zimbabwean dollars to buy the flour and she needed to make a lot more than that today to get a good return on her investment.

No one was in her favourite spot near the town gates when she arrived. Good! Soon, her large baskets of small loaves were displayed in a neat row by the roadside, decorated with brightly coloured cloth to entice customers as they entered the main marketplace in search of a bargain. (Hungry people aren't always fussy about the price when it comes to filling their bellies at early dawn.) She pulled out her sunshade and folding footstool, sat down, took a swig from a bottle of water and began the long wait for customers.

It was still quiet at the moment. Perhaps she should have brought a book to read—but no, it was like fishing, really. Her father had once taken her on a fishing trip to the river, and most of the day had been spent baiting hooks, casting lines, waiting for a bite… and then doing it all over again lots of times, for the rest of the day. As a child, Femi couldn't see the point. What did her father get out of it? They'd hardly caught anything!

But now she understood, because, years later, she was sitting here fishing for customers. Just like her father on the riverbank, she had to be patient, sitting, waiting, because you could never know if a really good customer was just about to come around the corner—the rich sort who bought five loaves, didn't try to ask for a discount, and left you with several million dollars in your pocket. She had to stay alert, catching people's eyes as they passed by in ones and twos, inviting them over.

At last her first customer strolled up, an old man. She'd seen him here before.

'Good morning, sister,' he smiled. 'How much for two loaves?'

Her eyes lit up. 'Twenty million dollars!'

He sighed. 'Last week, it was 15 million.'

After telling the story, explain that money can become worthless if the prices keep going up all the time. This increase in prices is called **inflation**. When you get serious inflation, as in this story, it's very hard to run a business because your costs rise faster than the money you're making, and saving money becomes pointless. Despite this, people around the world, like Femi, still do their best and hope for a better future.

She nodded sadly. 'That was before the price of flour went up. But, brother, they taste so delicious and you need fattening up!'

He sighed, grinned, then pulled out his thick pack of million-dollar notes and carefully handed over 20 of them. 'I don't understand it,' he said, holding up one million-dollar note before putting it away again. 'When I was a child, a loaf of bread cost three shillings. Now it's millions of dollars. The money's gone crazy!'

'I know, brother,' Femi replied as she bagged up the loaves. 'I remember when bread was only a few hundred dollars for a loaf.'

'You're that young?' he said, winking, and strolled away.

Femi pocketed the notes. When younger, she'd always dreamed of one day becoming a millionaire, but now the money had gone crazy and everybody in her village was a millionaire. These days, a million dollars would only buy you an orange. Oh well. By the end of the day, she might be a multi-millionaire, a billionaire or even a trillionaire—and that would buy her a few extra bags of flour before the prices went up again.

Another customer was approaching, looking well-dressed. Femi smiled her best smile. 'Can I help you, sister?'

Reproduced with permission from *Valuing Money* by Chris Hudson (Barnabas in Schools, 2015) www.barnabasinschools.org.uk

Religious Education

Age 5–7: Making the most of what you've got

Both the following activities take the 'small business' theme further.

In the Christian Bible, Jesus describes a time when God will bring 'things as they are' to an end and reward his followers according to what they have done. In one famous parable, he likens the people of his time to the servants of a businessman (representing God) who sets them a challenge—to make a decent profit from the money he'd entrusted to them. Some come out of the challenge better than others.

This powerful idea has existed in human society for a very long time. The 'parable of the talents' shows people being encouraged to make the most of whatever skills and assets they have, to serve their master by doing business and increasing the value of those assets. If they lack confidence to do it themselves, they must at least have the intelligence to invest their resources with those who can increase the value.

Bible link: Matthew 25:14–30

The kingdom is also like what happened when a man went away and put his three servants in charge of all he owned. The man knew what each servant could do. So he handed five thousand coins to the first servant, two thousand to the second, and one thousand to the third. Then he left the country.

As soon as the man had gone, the servant with the five thousand coins used them to earn five thousand more. The servant who had two thousand coins did the same with his money and earned two thousand more. But the servant with one thousand coins dug a hole and hid his master's money in the ground.

Some time later the master of those servants returned. He called them in and asked what they had done with his money. The servant who had been given five thousand coins brought them in with the five thousand that he had earned. He said, 'Sir, you gave me five thousand coins, and I have earned five thousand more.'

'Wonderful!' his master replied. 'You are a good and faithful servant. I left you in charge of only a little, but now I will put you in charge of much more. Come and share in my happiness!'

Next, the servant who had been given two thousand coins came in and said, 'Sir, you gave me two thousand coins, and I have earned two thousand more.'

'Wonderful!' his master replied. 'You are a good and faithful servant. I left you in charge of only a little, but now I will put you in charge of much more. Come and share in my happiness!'

The servant who had been given one thousand coins then came in and said, 'Sir, I know that you are hard to get along with. You harvest what you don't plant and gather crops where you haven't scattered seed. I was frightened and went out and hid your money in the ground. Here is every single coin!'

The master of the servant told him, 'You are lazy and good-for-nothing! You know that I harvest what I don't plant and gather crops where I haven't scattered seed. You could have at least put my money in the bank, so that I could have earned interest on it.'

Then the master said, 'Now your money will be taken away and given to the servant with ten thousand coins! Everyone who has something will be given more, and they will have more than enough. But everything will be taken from those who don't have anything. You are a worthless servant, and you will be thrown out into the dark where people will cry and grit their teeth in pain.'

Use drama to act out the parable.

Warm up the class by encouraging them to pose as different 'feelings' in the story (rich and proud, confident, lacking confidence and so on).

Put them into three groups, each group representing one of the servants in the story. As the teacher, you play the businessman who sets the challenge of making as much money as possible from what he gives them. Each apprentice is secretly given a different sum of money (£5000, £2000 and £1000) and reacts to it. The one given the least cash should act the most frightened.

Each group acts out their responses in mime. Perhaps the first group could go into business by making things in a factory, and the next could become bakers. They might act out 'selling' their goods as local market traders. The last group (*'Oh no! What am I going to do?'*) simply buries the cash. When the businessman returns, the groups have to report back and are treated just like in the parable. Perhaps you can say, 'You're hired… you're hired… and *you're fired!*'

Discuss

Explain that this story is a picture of people being entrusted with a responsibility by God. Everybody has their own set of special skills and talents. Discuss the following questions.

- What was the businessman using his money to do?
- If you were the servant who'd been fired, what would you say at the end?
- What questions would you have for the businessman in charge?
- What do you think is the key message of this story?
- What might it mean for Christians?

Ask pupils to draw the three responses of the apprentices as quick cartoons in their exercise books, adding speech bubbles or faces to show their feelings regarding the challenge. They can note down what they think is the key message or the most interesting question.

Extension activity: discussion and writing

- What do we think our own skills and talents are?
- How could we use them to make life better for other people?

Age 8–11: The wise businesswoman

The Old Testament book of Proverbs, an ancient collection of wise sayings, ends with a portrait of a remarkable businesswoman. She is skilled in handling business and craft, successfully managing a workforce, a home and a family.

Bible link: Proverbs 31:10–31

A truly good wife is the most precious treasure a man can find! Her husband depends on her, and she never lets him down. She is good to him every day of her life, and with her own hands she gladly makes clothes.

Note

You could, if appropriate, refer to the BBC reality show *The Apprentice*, where aspiring businesspeople are given a series of challenges to evaluate their skills at making money. Every episode ends with a final judgement: which team was the most successful, and why?

She is like a sailing ship that brings food from across the sea. She gets up before daylight to prepare food for her family and for her servants. She knows how to buy land and how to plant a vineyard, and she always works hard. She knows when to buy or sell, and she stays busy until late at night. She spins her own cloth, and she helps the poor and the needy. Her family has warm clothing, and so she doesn't worry when it snows. She does her own sewing, and everything she wears is beautiful.

Her husband is a well-known and respected leader in the city. She makes clothes to sell to the shop owners. She is strong and graceful, as well as cheerful about the future. Her words are sensible, and her advice is thoughtful. She takes good care of her family and is never lazy. Her children praise her, and with great pride her husband says, 'There are many good women, but you are the best!'

Charm can be deceiving, and beauty fades away, but a woman who honours the Lord deserves to be praised. Show her respect—praise her in public for what she has done.

Ask pupils to study this passage in pairs, first listing all the verbs describing what the woman does, then describing what they think are her three key business skills.

Notice how verse 30 describes her as a woman who 'has respect for the Lord'. How might a person's religious faith affect the way they do business? How is that expressed in this passage? For example, is she likely to lie or cheat when she does business deals?

Discuss the impact the woman makes on her family and others. What do pupils think is the most important thing we can learn from her?

Ask the pupils to illustrate their responses to the passage by tracing around a hand, then listing or drawing near the fingers the five most important things that they think the woman does with the money she earns, to make life better for her family and other people. For extension, design one piece of jewellery for each finger, using different symbols and colours to represent each of these five things.

Numeracy

Age 5–7: Classroom shop

In the classroom, set up a shop with plastic money as currency and goods priced appropriately. Pupils should spend a certain amount of money as they wish, then record the transaction (including change received) as number sentences.

When everyone has done this, discuss which are the most popular goods, and why. Results could be displayed on a table or bar graph.

Raise the prices on the most popular products and repeat the experience. Discuss what happens. What did people want to do when they found that the price had gone up? List pupils' responses—for example, get more money, buy it anyway, buy something else, buy it somewhere else and so on.

Explain that it is called **inflation** when prices keep going up.

How would we feel if some children were given more or less money to start with? Why?

Age 8–11: Trading simulation games

Role play is an excellent way to immerse pupils in the dilemmas of making a living in an unfair world, and boys especially enjoy the element of competition. Development charities such as Christian Aid, CAFOD and Traidcraft all offer free financial role-play activities as downloads on their websites. When running these games, allow at least an hour per session, with plenty of time immediately afterwards for feedback and reflection on what it felt like when acting 'in character'. Talk about how it might affect pupils' own buying choices in future.

- The Orange Trading Game shows how trading conditions affect the incomes of citrus farmers.
  Go to www.traidcraftschools.co.uk and search for 'orange trading game'. (You'll find it under the heading 'Indoor activities'.)
- The Banana Split Game does the same for banana growers.
  Scroll down the page at www.oneworldweek.org/v2/downloadble-games.html.
- For cocoa growers, play the Chocolate Trade Game.
  http://learn.christianaid.org.uk/TeachersResources/primary/choc_trade.aspx
- The Paper Bag Game re-enacts how some streetchildren have to make money from turning scrap newspaper into bags.
  http://learn.christianaid.org.uk/TeachersResources/primary/pbag.aspx

Literacy

Age 5–11: Buy unfair trade!

Explain that fair trade works by encouraging the use of community projects that pay better rates to producers than they would receive through usual business practices. Set pupils the following tasks.

- Write some copy advertising a product that has been definitely unfairly traded!
- Design a 'Not-Fair Trade' logo and explain its message.

Geography

Age 5–11: Alternative world mapping

On the internet, search for 'alternative global maps' showing different measures of wealth, such as:

- personal income
- access to clean water
- percentage of primary-age children in the population who attend school
- life expectancy at birth

Discuss the maps with the class. What do we notice and what are the most interesting questions we can ask about them?

Design Technology

Age 5–11: Show some enterprise

Many primary schools have design-and-build projects in which pupils create products to sell at community events. Young Enterprise is just one charity offering free downloadable schemes of work to support a half-term's cross-curricular topic exploring the wider world of small businesses. See www.young-enterprise.org.uk.

Circle Time

Age 5–11: What do I enjoy doing, and why?

This is a session exploring the activities that give us pleasure.

Preparation

Be ready to talk about two personal enthusiasms from work and leisure. Are there related items you could show your pupils for illustration?

Introduction

Talk about two activities you personally enjoy doing in and out of school, and explain why.

Development

Ask pupils to think about all the things they enjoy doing, both in school and out of school. We're all different and our enthusiasms reveal something very important about us: they show how our minds work. It could be that we like challenges, discovering something new, being creative or doing things with other people.

Set pupils the task of listing with a partner two or three things they really enjoy doing, with reasons. Ask some (willing) pupils to feed back to the class. Explain that these enthusiasms are very important, and if we discover something we enjoy doing, we shouldn't forget it. Perhaps it's something we need to practise, because it could be very important for us when we're older. As we grow up, some of these enthusiasms might turn into something bigger—an important life skill, a hobby or even a job.

There was once a famous athlete, a runner named Eric Liddell, who won a gold medal in the 1924 Olympics. When he was asked why he enjoyed training so much, he replied, 'Because when I am running, I can feel God's pleasure in me!'

∞ Prayer ∞

Father God, I'm special, and you made me this way for a purpose. Thank you for all those things I enjoy doing. Help me to appreciate them more. Amen

• Thought for today •

What do I enjoy doing most of all?

Unit 2

Genuine currency and forgeries

Background for teachers

There are many different ways to steal money, but making your own cash is one of the most serious. For centuries, the creation of fake currency has been treated as a crime by the authorities.

The British Museum's Money Gallery contains a display of fake Roman silver denarii dating from the second century AD, next to some modern fake pound coins.

Forgery has sometimes incurred the death penalty, because putting false bank notes or coins into circulation threatens trust in the established currency. During World War II, there was a highly dangerous Nazi plot to flood Britain with fake pound notes. (The Nazis knew all about the terrors of inflation: it had brought them to power in Germany during the 1930s.) Great efforts are still made to prevent currency forgery, which is why the Royal Mint, where they produce the real thing, is one of the most heavily guarded sites in the country, and also why the creation of new legal notes or coins has to include hard-to-copy security features such as watermarks.

In 1699, King William III appointed a very famous scientist to hunt down the coin forgers, and so Isaac Newton began a new career as Master of the Royal Mint at the Tower of London. The story that follows is based on fact, despite being told in the style of a hardboiled 1940s American detective thriller.

Story: Isaac Newton, currency detective

Note

Teachers from schools in Northern Ireland will know that the name 'King Billy' has local associations with past history. If the name is a distraction from the main point of the lesson, just refer to him as 'the king'.

Visual aids

Images of King William III, Isaac Newton and a gold guinea of the time

The name's Newton. Isaac Newton. Occupation: Master of the Royal Mint. Speciality: tracking down fraudsters, forgers, clippers, smelters and anyone else making money out of the king's coin. And who gave me the job? That's Billy, the one with his head on the coins—King William the Third, we call him. He's the big cheese, the numero uno. And, one day in 1699, he called me in.

'Isaac,' he said, as we stood on the palace balcony overlooking the City of London. 'There's trouble at the Mint. Criminals out there are making their own money. There's forgers who can take any old metal and turn it into fake silver and gold. Clippers are snipping edges from solid silver coins, reducing their weight and size, but still passing them off as the real deal. It's a racket as old as time, Isaac, so I need your help to find these people—and stop them. Dead.'

Why did he ask me? Because… I'm Isaac Newton. I know the metal. I'm the cool cat who discovered gravity and the Three Laws of Thermodynamics, and I know who put the colours in the rainbow, so I can tell a fake gold guinea just by looking at it. So now I work for King Billy, and he trusts me. Let me tell you the story of just one night I spent as Master of the Mint—and believe me, I'll tell it like it was.

It was late one evening and there were still plenty of people out on the mean streets of Deptford, London—people determined to have a good time even if it meant being bad. Not the best time for a raid, you might say, but we needed to catch our criminals red-handed. It's no use raiding a forger's house when everybody's asleep. You need to find them making the fake coins, cooking up the metal, pouring it into moulds, shaking out the new money, filing the edges and checking each piece for imperfections before trying to pass it off as genuine.

My men weren't in uniform this evening, just street clothes. We were all moving silently, finding our way along the road in surreptitious ones and twos, with Big Erik carrying the heavy sledgehammer under his cloak, ready to take out the door of the house. We were armed with pistols and swords. Forgers can pay for protection and we didn't know who'd be waiting on the other side of that door. We'd need to be fast, too. Most forgers have their escapes ready planned—a secret trapdoor, a hidden window or a hole in the roof. If they hear us coming, it's a case of leave the hot metal and coins, grab your tools and moulds, and run. Because the tools are what you need to set up business again at a new address—and they do set up business again, amazingly quickly. Believe me.

It was nearly time. Clutching my dark lantern and pistol, I stood next to Big Erik in the shadows opposite our target, a house by a busy inn. I'd told my team to go in at the first chimes of midnight from the church bells at St Mary's, Bow. Some of them were in position along the street, with others stationed round the back. Then, in the distance, a peal of bells from St Mary's and… One! Erik lifted the hammer. Two! He swung it with a crunch into the door. Three! The others were by me, weapons drawn. Four! Another massive blow from the hammer. 'They've reinforced it!' someone shouted. Five. Another blow, a splintering noise, the sound of someone moving inside. 'GET IN THERE!' I shouted. Six. Another blow. Seven. And another. Nearly there! Eight… and the door was down. We piled inside, four of my team heading up the stairs, with myself and Erik taking the ground floor. Then the sounds of running and shouting above us, someone screaming and, down below, the smell of chemicals and burnt metal. 'FOUND IT!' I yelled.

We didn't need our dark lanterns. The large parlour-room was lit bright with candles, everything on display, a small forge still hot from cooking the metal, with moulds, tools and some freshly forged coins—golden guineas by the look of them—still warm on a table, like biscuits fresh from the oven. I tried picking one up and Ouch! I quickly dropped it in a bucket of water nearby, sucking my sore fingers. He'd been working here just now, but where was he? Where was the master forger?

Reproduced with permission from *Valuing Money* by Chris Hudson (Barnabas in Schools, 2015) www.barnabasinschools.org.uk

More shouting overhead, and the clomping of boots. My guards thumped their way back down the stairs and into the parlour with a frightened woman who was holding a bundle of rags. Then the bundle moved and yawned, and I saw a sleeping baby, wrapped up against the cold.

'Where is he?' I demanded, waving my hand at the items on the bench. 'The one all this belongs to?' She looked puzzled, confused. I tried again. 'Where's the one who's been forging these coins?' I reached into the bucket, showed her the fake guinea, tested it with a bite, then spat on the floor. Real gold doesn't taste like that, trust me. But she knew nothing, of course. Yes, she owned the house, but the downstairs rooms were rented out to 'someone who always paid their rent on time and was no trouble, sir'.

'What did he pay you with?' I asked. She pulled a purse from her belt and showed me some coins. Not golden guineas of course—that would be far too much for a single room in Deptford. He'd been here earlier, I could smell it, and now he wasn't. But she had no idea where he'd gone. Then the baby decided to wake up, and, merciful heavens, was he hungry and angry and loud! I sighed.

Was there a hidden way into the inn next door? Erik checked the walls, hitting them with a stick and listening to the sound... and yes, there it was, behind a curtain. A false section of hollow wall. I stepped over, tapped it with my fist, and behold, it swung away to reveal a room in the Dog and Duck and some rather puzzled drinkers staring back. 'Did you see anything?' I demanded. 'Anyone coming through this wall?'

'Of course not,' they said, turning back innocently to their drinks with a few smirks. I sighed. My guards found some planks and nailed it all shut as I wrote down the landlady's story, while her baby's screaming grew louder and louder. Finally, after bagging up all the tools, moulds and metal, I sent mother and baby back to bed and returned with my team to the Tower of London.

'So how do you know it wasn't her?' asked His Majesty. It was our weekly meeting, and I was telling him about the raid.

'A woman, Your Majesty?' I replied. 'Impossible! Where would a mere woman get the knowledge to forge coins?'

'Mr Newton,' he smiled, 'where did you get your own talents? People can forge almost anything if they put their minds to it. My enemies even say I forged my way into becoming king. I wonder where that lady and her baby are now. I suspect you'll find they've moved house already—and, curiously, no one will know where they are.'

Later that day I checked, and he was right, of course. She had disappeared. His Majesty was always better at reading people than me. But I do know my metals, and those forged coins we found at the house were very good. The supposed golden guineas even had the tiny elephant and castle inscribed under the king's head, to look like African gold coins, and I've kept the moulds in my private museum. So I'll keep watch. And, trust me, whoever made those coins—one day, I'll get him... or her!

Reproduced with permission from *Valuing Money* by Chris Hudson (Barnabas in Schools, 2015) www.barnabasinschools.org.uk

Religious Education

Age 5–7: Fake money, fake people

Note

Although intended as a general warning for children, this session might lead to a pupil making a disclosure about abuse. If that happens, staff must deal with it in line with the school's child protection policy.

Show some examples of obvious fake coins, such as the plastic coins you use in Numeracy or the chocolate money on sale at Christmas. Ask what would happen if we tried to spend them in a shop. Explain that real coins are designed to look special so that nobody can mistake anything else for the real thing. Ask how we would know that a coin was real. (The Queen's head on one side, the metal it's made from, mass/weight, shape, and so on.)

Show a real pound coin. Explain that it's against the law to make coins yourself, but some people still do it—and one in 30 of our pound coins is probably a fake. (If possible, pass round a fake pound coin or an image from an internet search.) For clues to spotting a fake in your change, go to www.royalmint.com/discover/uk-coins/counterfeit-one-pound-coins.

Explain that the fake coin 'says' it's worth a pound, but that's not true. It's worth very little, unless people believe it's real. Telling lies about what's real leads to trouble, but how can we tell what's real and true? By comparing the fake to the original and by listening to the advice given by the people who make the real thing.

Visual aids

Fake coins, real pound coin, mask

Jesus once told his followers to be careful of anyone claiming to be better than they were. Some people, he said, were like Greek actors ('hypocrites') putting on a mask *(display an image)* to perform a play—making a show of being good while playing a kind of game that was selfish, cruel and unkind. Like the coin, they were putting on a show but were actually fakes. How could someone tell the difference? By noticing not what they said, but what they actually did. (Were they really kind to others or not?) Jesus used picture-language to describe these people (see Matthew 7:13–19; 23:1–12), saying they were like:

- wolves dressed up as sheep, prowling around looking for victims
- fruit trees that only produce rotten fruit
- decorated graves ('whitewashed tombs'), which are beautiful to look at, but only from the outside

Note

Say that adults should always protect children. If one adult treats us in a way that frightens us or makes us feel uncomfortable, we must always tell another adult whom we know we can trust.

Pupils should then choose from the following tasks.

- Design an obviously fake coin that couldn't be spent on anything.
- Draw a person who is saying one thing but doing the exact opposite.
- Write about a time when someone you trusted let you down. What happened next?

Ask the pupils to copy this line underneath their drawing or writing:

Jesus said, 'You will know the truth, and the truth will set you free' (John 8:32).

Age 7–11: False advertising claims

Discuss: do any of us know someone who has been cheated out of some money?

In the Christian Bible, one of God's commandments says, 'Do not steal' (Exodus 20:15). What excuses might people use to claim that it's all right to steal? Discuss in pairs, then feed back.

Explain that financial crimes are known as **fraud**. Anyone making and using fake money is defrauding the public and the government, so the police take it really seriously. Long before the invention of coins and banknotes, the Old Testament writers declared that anyone using false weights and measures to defraud their customers was angering God too, because their trickery was making money out of lies.

Bible links: Deuteronomy 25:13–14; Proverbs 11:1; Proverbs 16:11; Proverbs 20:10; Micah 6:11

Don't try to cheat people by having two sets of weights or measures, one to get more when you are buying, and the other to give less when you are selling.

The Lord hates anyone who cheats, but he likes everyone who is honest.

The Lord doesn't like it when we cheat in business.

Two things the Lord hates are dishonest scales and dishonest measures.

But I, the Lord, will punish you for cheating with weights and with measures.

Some product advertising can be another type of trickery. The Trade Descriptions Act of 1968 makes it illegal to advertise something in a way that misleads consumers, but that doesn't mean people don't try it on, especially on the internet.

When he sent his followers out on a mission, Jesus said, 'I am sending you like lambs into a pack of wolves. So be as wise as snakes and as innocent as doves' (Matthew 10:16).

Ask pupils to use Jesus' metaphorical descriptions of the four animals to illustrate an instructional article or mini-poster entitled 'Beware! It's a money jungle out there', containing tips on spending your money wisely and not being tricked.

Literacy

Age 5–11: Misleading advertising

Using a range of evocative verb phrases, adverbs and adjectives, pupils should compose some enticing marketing text of up to 50 words, advertising a famous product such as a popular chocolate bar. It should include up to three hidden untruths designed to cheat the customer, such as false promises about what it will do or supposed special offers. Once they have finished, the pupils can set each other the challenge of spotting the false claims.

IT extension

Pupils can use a graphics programme to produce appropriate layout and images to accompany the text as an advertisement for a magazine or the web.

Numeracy/Science

Age 5–11: Finding fake coins

Modern coin-sorting machines or meters often rely on a coin's size, mass and level of magnetism to establish whether it is fake or not. Using a ruler, a set of scales (mechanical or digital) and a magnet, pupils should find out the actual dimensions, weights/mass and degree of magnetism for a range of real modern British (or euro) coins. If possible, include a fake coin in the range. Are the pupils able to spot it?

Citizenship

Age 7–11

Explain that local Trading Standards Officers have the job of checking that no one is sold goods or services based on lies. Food packaging has to tell the truth about what's inside, adverts mustn't say what's not true, and, if someone performs a job for us, then it has to be done well.

Traders who break the law are taken to court and punished if found guilty. If possible, share and discuss real examples from a local newspaper.

Circle Time

Age 5–11: Why is trust so important?

This is a session about why being trustworthy is crucial in any community.

Preparation

Provide a chair and space to move around.

Introduction

Who thinks that they can be trusted? Who thinks teachers can be trusted? Stage a trust experiment with a willing volunteer. The volunteer stands with their back to you and a chair behind their legs, but not touching. You stand behind the chair and hold its back firmly, lifting it slightly above the ground. Ask the volunteer to shut their eyes and sit down quickly on the chair without using their hands, when you give a verbal signal. Do they trust you not to whip away the chair? Praise them for their help, either way!

Tell the class not to conduct this experiment with their friends without a responsible adult to supervise them. Accidents hurt people!

Development

What does it mean if you say you trust someone? (You are relying on them not to hurt you or tell you a lie.)

Ask the class: since waking up this morning, what have you been trusted by other people to do? Discuss the answers. Then ask: what have you trusted other people to do? Discuss, and list the answers together.

What would happen if you couldn't be trusted or if you couldn't trust other people to do these things? (Life might be a lot more difficult or dangerous.)

Explain that we live in a time and place where most people can be trusted to say and do the right thing, most of the time—but, if someone lets us down, we might not feel so safe afterwards. If you don't feel safe about something, what should you do? (Tell a responsible adult.) Trust helps us all to feel a lot safer, provided that everyone can be trusted.

What is it like in a class if just one person starts secretly stealing things or messing something up? Discuss.

If somebody starts to mess about in the toilets when no one is watching, how does their behaviour affect everybody else? If you saw someone doing it, what might go through your mind? Discuss.

Explain that it only takes a few people secretly being selfish to mess things up for everybody else— because then it's harder to trust people. That's why it's so important to tell the truth. If we are buying things, we need to know that the other person isn't trying to cheat us, selling us something we don't want. If people are honest, then everyone feels safer, because there is more trust about—so we should all try to stay trustworthy by being reliable and honest.

∞ Prayer ∞

Father God, help me to be someone who can be trusted by other people, so that they feel safe with me. Amen

· Thought for today ·

Trust is like glue: it holds people together.

Unit 3

A source of security

Background for teachers

How much should a government spend on keeping a country secure? How much should we spend on our own home security?

China's first great emperor, Qin Shi Huang, was intelligent, ambitious and ruthless—prepared to do anything to keep his own life and throne safe. As a result, the country's vast resources were poured into capital projects that unified the kingdom, at great cost in money and lives. The remains of many of Qin's projects still exist today, including examples of the first unified currency, featuring those classic round coins with a square hole (*yuan*), which symbolised the Middle Kingdom surrounded by the circle of heaven. The emperor's obsession with survival led to the creation of the famous life-size 'terracotta warriors' buried beside his tomb, serving as spiritual imperial guardians to accompany him into the next life. The archaeologists who discovered them were initially puzzled by one detail: why did so many of the warriors appear to be lacking the weapons that must have been buried with them? It is now thought that they were pillaged by rebels seeking the means to overthrow the emperor's son who succeeded him. If so, they were successful: the son didn't last long.

Two hundred years later, in a small country at the other end of the trade route from China (a route now known as the Great Silk Road), the young rabbi Jesus of Nazareth taught parables about the insubstantial security of material possessions. His audience was only too familiar with other apparently secure kingdoms that didn't last. So, when he told them to seek God's kingdom first, it wasn't wishful thinking, just good sense.

Story: The Emperor of the Earth Dragon

I wonder… what could go wrong if you had everything you wanted?

Long ago and far away, in a vast land that would one day be named 'China', there was a young man who wanted to be lord of everything he could see from the top of a high mountain. His name was Prince Qin Shi Huang. By the age of 13, he had become king of the great province of Quin. Others plotted to kill him and take his place, but he was too cruel and crafty to allow it—and so they died instead of him, often quite painfully. Poison is like that.

Qin Shi Huang wanted more, so he sent his army out to fight the bandit peoples who lived in the north and west, beyond the borders of his land. After his warriors had won their battles, with much shedding of blood, he sent them east and south of his kingdom to fight even more. The fighting was cruel and without mercy. Thousands died but, by the end, Qin Shi Huang was Emperor of the great Middle Kingdom of China. At the age of 37, he was now the richest and most powerful man in history and, as far as he was concerned, his empire was the centre of the whole world.

But how could he remain Emperor? By now, Qin had made many enemies. There were families who had lost loved ones, powerful people, their own eyes lusting after the Dragon Throne. Far behind them were many more, all awaiting their chance to charge over the borders of his kingdom with their armies to claim China for themselves. How could he control them all and stay alive?

Qin was a man of ideas, so he decided to keep his people busy, forcing them to work for years on massive building projects paid for with high taxes, wearing them out with long lists of commands and demanding that everybody kept a close watch on everybody else. No one was allowed to have weapons, unless they were members of the Imperial Guard. Any captured weapons were melted down, either to be forged into great bells that rang out on the Emperor's birthday or to be turned into vast statues of the Emperor himself, so that everyone remembered who was really in charge.

Qin also ordered a great collecting-in of books, the sort of books that encouraged people to ask awkward questions. The pages were burnt in town marketplaces across the land as a warning to everyone to be careful what they read—and not to think too much, or they might end up like the people who wrote those books…

After that, thousands of soldiers and labourers were sent to construct long straight roads linking up the great proud cities of the kingdom, bringing every territory within fast marching distance of his guards. Now, no one was beyond the Emperor's reach. Then they began building a massive defensive wall, the first Great Wall of China, stretching along the borders for thousands of miles, like a giant scaly earth dragon that had given up flying and flopped, exhausted, to the ground.

But still the Emperor was frightened. Despite his best efforts, he did not feel safe, because he knew that one day he would die—and the thought filled his days and nights with horror. Qin Shi Huang believed in ghosts and spirits, and he was terrified that, on the day he died, the spirits of all the people he had killed or worked to death would be waiting to punish him. What could he do?

So he decided not to die. Somewhere in the world, surely there had to be some magic elixir of life that would help the great Emperor Qin Shi Huang to live for ever. He began paying explorers and magicians to search for the secret of eternal life. He drank special medicines that the magicians promised would keep him healthy, but none of them worked. Finally, after a long and painful sickness, the Emperor died, hated by everyone. He was buried in a vast underground tomb, surrounded by an army of 8000 terracotta clay warriors to protect him from the spirits of his enemies. One of his sons then became the new Emperor, but within a year he was dead, too. Why? Because the people had seen enough Emperors of the Earth Dragon and didn't want any more—at least, not for now.

Qin Shi Huang was rich in so many ways, but I wonder… was he also poor? What do you think?

Reproduced with permission from *Valuing Money* by Chris Hudson (Barnabas in Schools, 2015) www.barnabasinschools.org.uk

Religious Education

Age 5–7: Rich towards God?

Ask the class to imagine being so rich that they can do anything they want—but they have no friends or family they can trust. What would they do to make life better? Discuss.

Jesus told a story of a rich farmer who built up a fortune and then stockpiled his wealth in hope of a long, comfortable retirement. Hoarding grain was thought to be a highly selfish kind of speculation. Rich businessmen could make money from famines by waiting for the price to go up through scarcity, then selling their grain at home or abroad, making a 'killing' from the desperate hunger of others.

Bible link: Luke 12:15–21

> Then he said to the crowd, 'Don't be greedy! Owning a lot of things won't make your life safe.'
>
> So Jesus told them this story.
>
> A rich man's farm produced a big crop, and he said to himself, 'What can I do? I don't have a place large enough to store everything.'
>
> Later, he said, 'Now I know what I'll do. I'll tear down my barns and build bigger ones, where I can store all my grain and other goods. Then I'll say to myself, "You have stored up enough good things to last for years to come. Live it up! Eat, drink, and enjoy yourself."'
>
> But God said to him, 'You fool! Tonight you will die. Then who will get what you have stored up?'
>
> This is what happens to people who store up everything for themselves, but are poor in the sight of God.

Read or share the story in your own words, or act it out.

As a class, discuss what other good things the farmer might have done with his money instead of keeping it all for himself. (Note that he didn't keep the farm going. When he retired, did he put all his farm labourers out of work?)

Ask the pupils to imagine they have £100 to spend, but not on themselves. What might be the best things you could do with the money?

Pupils could draw and label the 'rich fool' sitting in a room surrounded by his money. Outside his house, they could draw some things he could spend his money on, that might do other people a lot more good, along with a sand-timer running out of sand. Jesus told his followers to be 'rich towards God'. What do the pupils think that might have meant for his followers then? What might it mean for Christians now?

Age 7–11: Power and temptation

In the story of the temptations in the wilderness, the devil tempts Jesus to abandon his mission, by suggesting alternative ways to show his power. As a bribe, he offers him 'all the kingdoms on earth and their power'. So, with all his talents, Jesus is being offered the chance to become an incredibly rich and powerful emperor of the world, if he plays by the devil's rules.

Bible link: Matthew 4:1–11

The Holy Spirit led Jesus into the desert, so that the devil could test him. After Jesus had gone without eating for forty days and nights, he was very hungry. Then the devil came to him and said, 'If you are God's Son, tell these stones to turn into bread.'

Jesus answered, 'The Scriptures say: "No one can live only on food. People need every word that God has spoken."'

Next, the devil took Jesus to the holy city and had him stand on the highest part of the temple. The devil said, 'If you are God's Son, jump off. The Scriptures say: "God will give his angels orders about you. They will catch you in their arms, and you won't hurt your feet on the stones."'

Jesus answered, 'The Scriptures also say, "Don't try to test the Lord your God!"'

Finally, the devil took Jesus up on a very high mountain and showed him all the kingdoms on earth and their power. The devil said to him, 'I will give all this to you, if you will bow down and worship me.'

Jesus answered, 'Go away Satan! The Scriptures say: "Worship the Lord your God and serve only him."'

Then the devil left Jesus, and angels came to help him.

Share the story using artwork or other media.

In class, discuss and write about some of the following questions.

- Suppose Jesus had given in to the temptations. What different things might have happened next? What are your most interesting questions about this story?
- How could getting what we want be bad for us and for others?
- Can we think of other stories or films that include a scene where someone has a choice similar to the one Jesus had to make? (For example, responses to the Ring in *Lord of the Rings* or *The Hobbit*.)
- In a dictionary, look up the words 'temptation' and 'sin'. Are they both the same thing? Christians believe that temptation is different from sin. What do you think?
- Jesus used memorised bits of the Bible to help him resist the devil. Do we know of any famous sayings that could help us do the right thing when we're not sure?
- What temptations do people face today? How do you think people can resist temptation? Write and draw your thoughts on these questions.
- What could this story be saying about money and the things it can do for us?

Numeracy

Age 7–11

Set the following problems for pupils to solve.

- Jiangshi is a large town in China at the time of the First Emperor, with a population of 3573 people. The emperor has declared that there should be one member of his Imperial Guard to watch every eight people in the town. How many guards will be needed? What interesting questions would you like to ask about this law?

- The First Emperor's palace has 112 bedrooms. Imagine he sleeps in a different room every night so that it is harder for an assassin to find and kill him. How many weeks and days will it take before he has to sleep in any room for a second time?

- You are a modern archaeologist, reconstructing terracotta warriors from fragments you have discovered. In all, you have found 35 legs and 20 arms. How many heads and torsos are you looking for? What pieces might be left over? Is there more than one possible answer?

History

Age 7–11

Set your pupils the following tasks.

- Research the story of Qin Shi Huang, China's First Emperor, the building of the First Great Wall and the creation, burial and rediscovery (in 1974) of the terracotta army. Create a short report or mini-poster listing the main things that the emperor did.

- Research the lives of Sarah Winchester and Mikhail Kalashnikov, who were both made incredibly rich by the production of weapons but appear to have regretted it later. Compare the key points of their lives. What is similar and different about these two stories? (See en.wikipedia.org/wiki/Sarah_Winchester and en.wikipedia.org/wiki/Mikhail_Kalashnikov.)

Circle Time

Age 5–11: What does 'responsible' mean?

This is a session encouraging pupils to think about their own responsibilities.

Preparation

Find pictures of Peter Pan (preferably one of the pre-Disney illustrations), Qin Shi Huang (China's first Great Emperor) and Jesus in the wilderness.

Introduction

Ask, 'Who has heard the story of Peter Pan?' (Recount some key plot details, drawing out the fact that he is a boy who never grows up.) Describe the very sad bit at the end of the original story when Peter comes back to play with the children—only to find that they've all grown up. He is trapped, because he's always going to be the same. Peter never grows up.

Development

Remind pupils of the story of the First Great Emperor of China. When he was young, Qin Shi Huang decided he wanted to become emperor at any cost. Ask them to think, too, about the story of Jesus in the wilderness, tempted to have whatever he wanted. He said no, because he wanted to serve God in a better way. Both these people were facing the question, like in the made-up story of Peter Pan: what do you want to do for the rest of your life? They all chose differently.

Ask, 'Who here wants to grow up? Why?' Discuss in pairs and feed back to the class.

Ask, 'What are the three main things you're looking forward to being able to do, when you're grown up?' Discuss in pairs, then feed back to the class.

Explain that growing up isn't just about getting bigger and older. It's also about learning to become responsible. This morning, what did the pupils have to 'make happen' when they got up? What things do they have to 'make happen' when they come to school? That's what responsibility means.

As we get older, we're trusted to do more things. People who can handle these choices well then get trusted with even more things, because they've got a greater sense of responsibility. Jesus said, 'Everyone who has something will be given more, and they will have more than enough' (Matthew 25:29).

Growing up is about learning how to handle responsibility. That includes learning to handle money well, and it can be a bit scary. Some people don't like making choices: they prefer to have someone else make their decisions for them, someone to blame when things go wrong. If we want to grow up well, we need to think about what we're responsible for now and do it well—or we might be a bit like Peter Pan.

∞ Prayer ∞

Ask the pupils to close their eyes and imagine themselves grown up, doing something really important, something that others are trusting them to do well. Now ask them to think harder. What are they going to do today in school that could help them become that person in future?

Father God, thank you that we can grow older and wiser and cleverer every day. Amen

· Thought for today ·

What am I responsible for in class today?

Unit 4

Symbols and power statements

Background for teachers

Every coin and banknote carries a range of messages about the authority that issues it. The messages are partly to declare that the coin or note is worth what it says, but they also underline the power and worth of whoever makes and distributes the currency. Coins were first minted in the Middle East around 700BC, stamped with symbols depicting their city of origin. By 300BC, they were featuring heads of state in idealised representations looking left or right, creating the common pattern that has functioned ever since as a subtle form of official propaganda.

This is why the Women's Social and Political Union began defacing coins as a political gesture in the early 20th century. The WSPU were always highly creative when spreading their message demanding the right to vote for women. The 'Emily' in this story (Emily Wilding Davison) was later killed at the 1912 Epsom Derby while making a different type of public protest: it is now thought that she was trying to attach a suffragette symbol to the king's horse as it rode by. The defacing of coins was a considerably safer tactic, but, in its own way, just as subversive.

Story: A penny for your thoughts

Note

Defacing official coinage or notes is still against the law of the United Kingdom. You have been warned…

Emily was early. She had been looking forward to this meeting, arriving at Christabel Pankhurst's house just after supper. Christabel welcomed her warmly, asked a few questions, then showed her into a large room with a long wooden table in the middle, covered with tools.

'Now, Emily, this is where it all happens. Do you have a penny in your purse?' Emily found one. 'Have a look at it,' said Christabel. 'I mean a good long look. Study it. Tell me what you see.'

Like everyone else, Emily handled pennies every day of her life, but never looked at them closely. Why bother? Wasn't a penny just a penny? One side of the coin showed Britannia, a proud woman sitting on a throne, facing the right and holding a spear, with a Union Jack shield. On the other side lay the profile of King Edward VII, staring off to the right as well. She held the coin up to the light to read the tiny capital letters:

EDWARDVS VII DEI G. A. BRITT. OMN: REX FID: DEF: IND IMP:

'What do they mean?' asked Emily. 'Is it Latin?'

'Let me help you,' said Christabel. 'Let's see… you're right, it's Latin, and it means… 'Edward the Seventh, by the Grace of God, King of all the British territories, Defender of the Faith, and Emperor of India'. Quite a lot for a penny to carry, don't you think? Do you understand what this coin is saying?'

Emily shook her head.

'It's saying that King Edward VII is in charge! His people run the country and his people rule the world—well, a lot of it, anyway. And Emily, have you noticed? All of these rulers are men! We're ruled by a bunch of men who don't care about women. They don't think we need a decent education, they don't believe we should go out to work and they definitely don't think any women are sensible enough to vote at election time!'

Emily took the coin back, staring at the letters again, puzzled. 'But isn't this just a penny?'

Christabel's eyes flashed with anger. 'No, Emily! It's a symbol. It's a message being silently spoken every time we spend this money. It says Edward's on his throne and that's how things are going to stay. If he's got any sons, they'll be next. If he's got any girls, they'll just have to wait their turn until the boys are dead.'

Emily frowned. 'But we had Queen Victoria, didn't we?'

'Yes, but only because they didn't have any boys left! It's a man's world, Emily…' Christabel held up the coin, pointing at King Edward. 'That man's world! So we're going to use these pennies to send him a message.' She led Emily over to the table where there was a pile of hammers and a tray of metal rods looking something like thick pencils. She picked out one of the rods, which had a large capital letter V inscribed at its base. 'It's a letter punch—see? Pass me your penny.'

Christabel placed the coin on the table, held the punch over it and picked up a large hammer… which she raised and brought down with a WHACK! The penny now had a large 'V' stamped near the bottom of King Edward's head. 'See?' She picked up another coin from a basket marked 'FINISHED'. On this coin, a series of slightly wobbly capital letters spelled out (across King Edward's head) the words 'VOTES FOR WOMEN'.

Emily gasped. 'That's illegal, isn't it? Defacing the king's coinage. We're messing up his face.'

'That's the idea,' Christabel said, grinning. 'From now on, every person who uses that penny will see what we're saying, and maybe pass it on to somebody else. King Edward here's going to help

Reproduced with permission from *Valuing Money* by Chris Hudson (Barnabas in Schools, 2015) www.barnabasinschools.org.uk

us tell people that some of us are fed up with the way things are, and we're not going away and we're not going to keep quiet. Something's got to change. So, Emily… will you join us?'

Emily nodded, picked up another hammer, found the punch with a letter 'O' on it and started completing the coin that Christabel had started. She was soon loudly stamping her own way through a pile of pennies as other women joined them in the room to keep up the good work. This was going to be a long, noisy night, Emily thought—but, in her opinion, definitely worth it.

Reproduced with permission from *Valuing Money* by Chris Hudson (Barnabas in Schools, 2015) www.barnabasinschools.org.uk

Religious Education

Explain that coins and bank notes usually carry messages saying who is in charge of the money—rather like the sign outside a school that tells you who the head teacher is. Illustrate this with images of two or three obvious examples from modern currencies.

Age 5–7: 'The earth belongs to the Lord'

Share the following psalm with the class, omitting verses 3–6 (the second block of lines) if you wish. This song-poem was written by King David for people to sing as they came to worship God. In it, he declares that the whole world (not just his own country) is owned by the Lord God. David wants his people in the city of Jerusalem to welcome God into their lives and worship him.

Bible link: Psalm 24

> The earth and everything on it belong to the Lord.
> The world and its people belong to him.
> The Lord placed it all on the oceans and rivers.
>
> Who may climb the Lord's hill
> or stand in his holy temple?
> Only those who do right for the right reasons,
> and don't worship idols or tell lies under oath.
> The Lord God, who saves them, will bless and reward them,
> because they worship and serve the God of Jacob.
>
> Open the ancient gates,
> so that the glorious king may come in.
>
> Who is this glorious king?
> He is our Lord, a strong and mighty warrior.
>
> Open the ancient gates,
> so that the glorious king may come in.
>
> Who is this glorious king?
> He is our Lord, the All-Powerful!

Set the challenge of designing a bank note that says, 'The earth and everything on it belong to the Lord', which David might want people to use. You might include images of the globe, the creatures that live in it, and possibly a city on a hill. Since David was a shepherd-boy at first, there could be images associated with shepherding, or a crown symbolising the Lord as king.

Discuss

- Do you think that putting a special message on a coin or banknote could change the way we spent it?
- How might King David's message affect the way people spent their money, if they believed as he did?

Age 7–11: Giving back to Caesar

Jesus' enemies once asked him a question about money, to trick him into giving a politically incorrect answer: 'Should we pay taxes to the emperor or not?' The Roman occupation taxes were deeply unpopular with the Jewish people. If Jesus replied 'Yes', he would be unpopular with the people, but if he said 'No', he could be arrested by the authorities. Jesus famously said something else. His answer suggests two kingdoms at work—the kingdom of the emperor Caesar and the kingdom of God.

Bible link: Matthew 22:15–22

The Pharisees got together and planned how they could trick Jesus into saying something wrong. They sent some of their followers and some of Herod's followers to say to him, 'Teacher, we know that you are honest. You teach the truth about what God wants people to do. And you treat everyone with the same respect, no matter who they are. Tell us what you think! Should we pay taxes to the Emperor or not?'

Jesus knew their evil thoughts and said, 'Why are you trying to test me? You show-offs! Let me see one of the coins used for paying taxes.' They brought him a silver coin, and he asked, 'Whose picture and name are on it?'

'The Emperor's,' they answered.

Then Jesus told them, 'Give the Emperor what belongs to him and give God what belongs to God.' His answer surprised them so much that they walked away.

Retell this story, showing pupils an image of the Roman coin (a silver denarius) that Jesus might have used.

Set the task of quickly drawing the coin, then adding a speech bubble emanating from Caesar's mouth, saying what the Romans might demand from the people they rule. (Obey? Pay your taxes? Support the Empire? Join the legions?)

Ask, 'What might be the most important things, for Christians, that they think God wants them to do?' When Jesus was asked this question, he replied, 'Love God, and love your neighbour as you love yourself' (see Mark 12:30–31).

Invite pupils to design a Jesus coin. What key message might be written around the edge? What symbols or motifs might be included to represent part of the message? Should an image of Jesus himself be on the coin at all—or should there be something else?

Extension

Emily's protest campaign with the WSPU led to her frequently being arrested. During a sustained hunger strike in Holloway prison, she wrote, 'Rebellion against tyrants is obedience to God.' Tyrants are cruel rulers who do exactly what they like. Like many other women, Emily had decided that the only possible way to spread the WSPU message was by breaking the rules. Some members took it further by becoming violent, burning down buildings and attacking famous people.

Do you think this was right? How does it fit with these words of Jesus: 'Put your sword away. Anyone who lives by fighting will die by fighting' (Matthew 26:52).

How do you think a Christian or other religious believer today would react to being told that the only way to spread a message was by doing something violent?

Numeracy

Age 7–11

A penny was worth a lot more in 1900 than it is today. In this pre-decimal currency, there were 240 pennies to a pound, with 12 pennies to a shilling and 20 shillings to a pound. Set pupils the challenge of generating and solving some maths money problems using this system. Prices and activities can be found at: http://nrich.maths.org/5892 and http://downloads.bbc.co.uk/schools/primaryhistory/lesson_plans/tbt_resource_pack.pdf

Discuss

Can pupils think of any good reasons why the United Kingdom finally chose to adopt decimal currency in 1971, following the lead of most of Europe and the USA?

Which currency system do they prefer, and why? Ask some older people for their reactions, too. (The author of this book was aged twelve at the time of decimalisation—and was extremely relieved. Maths lessons suddenly became a lot easier!)

Circle Time

Age 5–11: What does it mean to show courage?

This session is about being brave when other people are being unkind.

Preparation

Bring something that makes 'a beautiful sound' for you, such as a CD track or musical instrument.

Introduction

Play the sound of something that makes you feel good, and explain why you like it so much.

Ask the pupils, 'What's the most beautiful sound in the world to you? What's the most horrible sound in the world for you?'

Development

Explain that, sometimes, people make horrible sounds at other people. Do you remember the story of Emily and Christabel? They were fed up about the way they were treated as women. Sometimes they were called very bad names by people who disagreed with them.

Have you ever been called bad names? What did you feel like inside when it happened? Why do you think other people call each other bad names? Discuss in pairs—how you feel when it happens, and why people do it. Insults can make us feel dirty inside, because they stay in the mind afterwards.

Have you ever heard the saying, 'Sticks and stones may break my bones, but words will never hurt me'? It's not true. Words do hurt. Some of the worst bullying comes from words.

Discuss what choices we have if someone says something horrible to us. There are three things we can do when people call us names. We can do it back, which usually makes things worse. We can get something done about it, such as asking an adult for help, or we can ignore it—which is hard when you're angry (and it's right to be angry when this happens, because name-calling is wrong).

Share what has helped you to feel stronger when people say bad things about you. Re-emphasise that name-calling is never acceptable. Every person is incredibly special and precious—and that is more important than any insult.

In the Easter story, Jesus had all sorts of horrible insults thrown at him, but he didn't bother replying. He had more important things to think about and do, and, in the end, he proved his enemies wrong. The next time someone uses cruel words, think, 'What's really going on here? What can I do about it that will make things better?' You could even ask, 'What would Jesus do?'

∞ Prayer ∞

Father God, I feel horrible inside when people say nasty things to me. Help me to remember that, to you, I'm a superstar. Amen

· Thought for today ·

Remember: next time you point a finger at someone else, the other fingers are pointing right back at you!

Unit 5

Playing with money

Background for teachers

How do we teach children to handle a budget and spend wisely? Pocket money provides practical experience in the real world, and we can play trading games that model the adult ability to accumulate and spend. However, some of these games carry hidden and not-so-hidden messages depicting a harsh world of predatory winners and abject losers, which isn't necessarily true of real life. The story in this unit reveals how the game of Monopoly was originally designed by an anti-poverty campaigner as a satire on unfair business practices (not that you'd know it now).

We can model other ways of understanding how the world of money works. There are some excellent alternative economics trading games on the market, and some charities offer free downloads for schools (see page 52). They can all show our budding entrepreneurs of the future that 'winning the best deal' may have hidden consequences for others and possibly for themselves, too. For example, our coffee beans might come cheaper if there's a drop in the international wholesale price. That might seem good for us, but it's not good if we end up paying a great deal more to help poorer countries whose economies were destabilised by the price-drop. In a global economy, everyone is connected and there are times when simply allowing the free market to take its course can work out even more costly for everyone.

Story: It's not fair!

Visual aids

A Monopoly board and playing piece; internet-sourced images of 'The Landlord's Game'

Just imagine if all this money was real! Jamal was holding a thick wodge of golden £100 notes that had once belonged to his little sister and his mum. He'd collected the three orange properties: Bow Street, Marlborough Street and Vine Street. Now there were three big fat red hotels sitting on his properties and he was raking in the rent from the other players as they landed on them.

'That will be another £1500,' he said, grinning, as Labiba's little dog landed on Vine Street.

'NOOOOOOOOOOOOO!' she screamed.

'But that's the rent!' He showed her the numbers on the property card. 'See? You landed on my hotel. That's £1500, please.'

'But…' she spluttered, ' I was saving up to buy my houses on Mayfair.'

Jamal shook his head. 'That's the rules. £1500, please. Now!'

'IT'S NOT FAIR!' howled Labiba, jumping up and throwing down her last golden banknotes at him. 'I'M OUT!' With that, she stormed out of the lounge, pausing to turn and stick out her tongue at him before slamming the door behind her.

'Baby, it's only a game!' Mum called, as her daughter stomped up the stairs to sulk in her bedroom. Jamal snorted as they put the pieces back into the box. Why did his sister have to take it so personally? The game wasn't so much fun when people got cross about losing. He wasn't the one who threw the dice that landed her on Vine Street. Why couldn't she lose without getting cross? All by himself, he'd worked out that the orange streets were the best buy: they were cheap to build on, but charged high rents. His sister had gone for the dark blues, trying to build expensive houses on expensive properties, but nobody had landed on them. The game was all about managing your luck, taking a risk and squashing the others. That's life, isn't it? That's what his Uncle Raj had said once, and Uncle Raj was a businessman, too, which proved it.

But Mum was giving Jamal a look. 'You know, you could help your sister a bit. She never wins.'

'But it's all about winning, isn't it? That's why we play!'

Mum sighed, raising an eyebrow. 'I thought it was meant to be about having fun together as a family. Remember?' She paused for a moment, then added, 'Do you know how this game was invented? Look it up. You might be surprised.' That evening, Jamal went surfing the net in search of the game's inventor—and Mum was right.

He found out that Monopoly was originally invented by a Quaker Christian named Elizabeth Magie in the USA, over 100 years ago. It was first called 'The Landlord's Game', and Lizzie (as she liked to be called) designed it to show how cruel landlords made their money. It was all about buying property cheaply, then charging the tenants high rents—but, in her version, there was a 'land tax' rule that forced landlords to pay rent into a common fund and all the players owned the railway stations, the waterworks and the electric companies. Jamal shrugged. How could that work? But Lizzie wanted to make the world a fairer place, and her game was a way of explaining her views to others.

Jamal wondered what it would be like to play the game with different rules. Suppose you couldn't charge a player more than once for rent on any single property? Or suppose that, after collecting just three rents on a property, you had to sell it back to the bank? What if you set a kitchen timer for 30 minutes, shouted 'Earthquake!' when it rang, and all the houses and hotels got knocked down? What if you could write your own Chance and Community Chest cards? His brain started buzzing…

Reproduced with permission from *Valuing Money* by Chris Hudson (Barnabas in Schools, 2015) www.barnabasinschools.org.uk

The next weekend, as the rain outside pattered on the windows, he pulled out the game from a cupboard and went to find his sister. 'Fancy a go?'

'NO!' she scowled. 'You always win!'

'But I've got an idea for some new rules.' He told Labiba about how the game had changed over the years and how you could make up your own extra rules if you wanted. Her eyes sparkled with delight. Perhaps this was a game they could all play in a different way. They'd be in charge of the action—and it would be more fun!

After sharing the story, discuss whether any children in your class play board games and how they react to winning or losing. Point out that we can learn a lot from playing games with others, such as following rules, taking turns and handling the feelings of winning or losing. It's all about keeping things fair, but what happens if things aren't fair? What does fairness actually mean, anyway?

Reproduced with permission from *Valuing Money* by Chris Hudson (Barnabas in Schools, 2015) www.barnabasinschools.org.uk

Religious Education

These two RE sessions use drama to act out relevant stories from the Bible, so you'll need some space to move around.

Age 5–7: Stephen and the grumpy grannies

Bible link: Acts 6:1–7

Ask the pupils if any of them have grannies and if their grannies ever get grumpy. (All grown-ups get grumpy at times.) Explain that you're going to be using drama to explore another story about fairness, where some grannies were very grumpy about feeling left out.

Sit the pupils in two concentric circles of equal numbers, with the inner ring (the grannies) facing the outer ring (the first Christians).

Explain that long ago, the first Christians in the Roman Empire were very good at looking after their old people and those who were ill. In fact, they were famous for it.

Discuss what sort of help old people or ill people might need. Act out some of the suggestions.

As more people joined the church from different backgrounds, both Jews and Greeks, the number of those needing help got bigger. *(Repeat the acting, but faster, getting more stressed.)* Some of the people in charge of taking round meals started saying, 'I can't do this any more!' and mistakes were made. Some of the Greek grannies got missed out. They started moaning. *('Where's my kebab? I'm hungry! It's not fair!')*

So Simon Peter and the other first Christians got together. *('What do we do now?')* They prayed about it. *('Lord, have you got any ideas?')* Then, after praying and listening to God, they came up with a plan. *('Ah hah! We have a plan!')* They would pray again and select some really caring Greek members of the church to make sure that all the food and care was shared out fairly.

That's just what happened. A man called Stephen headed up the team. *(Pick a child to stand and be 'in charge'. Act out the sharing and caring again. Grannies say, 'Yum! Kebabs! Thank you!')* The numbers of people joining the church got bigger… and bigger… and bigger… and the grannies got a bit fatter—which was probably a good thing.

Discuss how we can treat people unfairly for all sorts of reasons, such as because they speak a different language, have a family that comes from somewhere else, look different, have a different faith or belief and so on. Can we think of any more examples?

Treating people unfairly for these reasons is called 'prejudice', and it's wrong. The first Christians believed that everybody was important to God and tried to live out their beliefs, which is why the church grew very fast across the Roman Empire.

Arrange pupils into pairs. Ask them to list five ways in which they are different from each other and five ways in which they are similar. They can then draw themselves, listing or drawing the similarities and differences, with the statement, 'Christians believe we are all different—and all special to God.'

Age 7–11: The cucumber plot

The Hebrew Bible's tale of Naboth's vineyard shows a rich landowner using slander and murder to arrange a land-grab. This episode forms part of a much larger story about the struggle for hearts and minds between a corrupt monarchy and a succession of prophets 'speaking God's truth to power'.

Run a warm-up acting game introducing character poses such as:

- A farmer who works hard
- A king who has tantrums
- An evil plotting queen
- A devious spy
- Someone who's discovered a terrible truth

Bible link: 1 Kings 21:1–16

Naboth owned a vineyard in Jezreel near King Ahab's palace.

One day, Ahab said, 'Naboth, your vineyard is near my palace. Give it to me so I can turn it into a vegetable garden. I'll give you a better vineyard or pay whatever you want for yours.'

Naboth answered, 'This vineyard has always been in my family. I won't let you have it.'

So Ahab went home, angry and depressed because of what Naboth had told him. He lay on his bed, just staring at the wall and refusing to eat a thing.

Jezebel his wife came in and asked, 'What's wrong? Why won't you eat?'

'I asked Naboth to sell me his vineyard or to let me give him a better one,' Ahab replied, 'and he told me I couldn't have it.'

'Aren't you the king of Israel?' Jezebel asked. 'Get out of bed and eat something! Don't worry, I'll get Naboth's vineyard for you.'

Jezebel wrote a letter to each of the leaders of the town where Naboth lived. In the letters she said:

Call everyone together and tell them to go without eating today. When they come together, give Naboth a seat at the front. Have two liars sit across from him and swear that Naboth has cursed God and the king. Then take Naboth outside and stone him to death!

She signed Ahab's name to the letters and sealed them with his seal. Then she sent them to the town leaders.

After receiving her letters, they did exactly what she had asked. They told the people that it was a day to go without eating, and when they all came together, they seated Naboth at the front. The two liars came in and sat across from Naboth. Then they accused him of cursing God and the king, so the people dragged Naboth outside and stoned him to death.

The leaders of Jezreel sent a message back to Jezebel that said, 'Naboth is dead.'

As soon as Jezebel got their message, she told Ahab, 'Now you can have the vineyard Naboth refused to sell. He's dead.' Ahab got up and went to take over the vineyard.

Use drama to tell the story. To keep everybody involved, the story could be acted out by four different groups of children playing the key protagonists: Naboth the vineyard owner, Ahab the king, Jezebel his queen, and the spies. The prophet Elijah can be played by a teacher.

Begin by getting each group (numbered 1, 2, 3 and 4) to act out the different stages of growing grapes and making wine. Take turns to clear stones, plough the land, spread manure, plant seedlings, water the plants, add more manure, watch them grow, prune some of the branches, pick the grapes, squash the juice in a large winepress, bottle the juice, leave it on a shelf, taste it... and then spit it out with a YUCK!

Get Group 1 to act out the working life of Naboth, whose vineyard produced grapes. Speed up the whole 'planting/growing/harvesting' process so it goes from seedling to wine in one minute—and this time, it tastes 'quite good, really'.

Group 2 should introduce themselves as King Ahab, who keeps a vegetable garden as a hobby. Act out growing cucumbers from seed to harvest to make a nice cucumber sandwich. One day, Ahab looks at his garden, thinks 'I need more land' and tries to buy the vineyard.

Naboth (Group 1) says, 'No, it's been in my family for generations! My father worked it, my grandfather worked it, we've all worked it. Sorry, Your Majesty, but no!'

Ahab tries increasing the cash offer, but Naboth refuses. This makes Ahab so angry that he sulks and sulks and sulks. ('It's not fair!')

Group 3 enter the story as Queen Jezebel, who was a very nasty woman. She was quite happy to murder anyone who got in her way. 'Darling, I'll take care of your garden,' she says, and, smiling prettily, starts writing letters. 'That'll sort it!' she exclaims, with an evil laugh.

Group 4 enter: the local citizens (the spies) receive Jezebel's letters, open them and exclaim, 'Oh no, I can't do that! But if I don't, she'll kill me!'

Next day, there is a town council meeting and Naboth is there. Jezebel's spies announce that a traitor has been selling the city's secrets to their enemies. They hold up letters saying, 'Here's the proof!' Naboth denies it, but is stoned to death (in mime, of course!).

The next day, King Ahab (Group 2 again) claims his garden. ('Oh dear, how sad. Never mind.') He rips up the vines and plants his cucumbers, adding manure to the soil—and then he hears a threatening voice.

Elijah the prophet (the teacher) appears, saying, 'Ahab, you're in deep trouble now! Ahab, you murdered a man and stole his property. See that manure? You're in it up to your neck! Because Naboth was murdered, you are going to die. God has spoken. He wants his world to be fair. You and your family are DOOMED!' (In the end, that was just what happened: see 1 Kings 22.)

Discuss

- What's the most interesting question you can ask about this story?
- What's the moral of the story?
- What do we think this story is saying about fairness?

Set pupils the task of retelling the key parts of the story as an eight-frame comic strip. You could use one sheet of A4 paper folded into eight rectangles.

Numeracy

Age 9–11: Monopoly

Board games such as Monopoly provide excellent opportunities for exercising fast calculation.

- Utilities charge fines of 'times four' or 'times ten' the number thrown on the dice. What are all the fines going to be for different dice throws on a range of 2 to 12?
- The dreaded Chance cards demanding 'repairs on all your properties' force property owners to pay out ten per cent on the value of each house or hotel. Set pupils the challenge of calculating ten per cent (or 15 per cent) on a range of properties (for example, three hotels on the 'reds' at £150 each).

Discuss

Everybody needs somewhere to live. In real life, landlords of rented properties and their tenants have to sign agreements promising to keep certain rules. What do you think the three most important rules on a 'tenancy agreement' ought to be for both sides?

Age 9–11: Monopoly with adapted rules

Any simulation game that claims to represent 'real life' has an inbuilt set of rules about how people win—usually by amassing more money, property or power than anyone else. Elizabeth Magie wanted to show children how rich people could make life harder for poor people by buying up cheap properties, charging higher and higher rents and making homeless anyone who couldn't pay—then using the money to buy even more property. Her idea ('The Landlord Game') was sold on to a games manufacturer, adjusted and rebranded as 'Monopoly'. It went on to be a great success around the world. Do games like this actually teach us to be greedy? Not necessarily—if you change the rules.

Try playing a simulation game using one or more of these adapted rules for Monopoly. How do they change the way you play?

- Set a time limit for the game instead of playing it until only one player is left.
- All fines must be placed in the middle of the board, to be won by anyone landing on Free Parking.
- No one is allowed to charge a rent higher than £400.
- Everyone must always be allowed to keep three properties.
- No one is allowed to own more than six properties in total.
- Include inflation, so that all property prices have to increase by ten per cent every 20 minutes.
- Invent and make your own cards for Community Chest and Chance. How about adding a Jubilee card that forces everybody to share out equally all the money they are holding?

More options can be found at: www.playagaingames.com/games/monopoly/home_rules.

Circle Time

Age 5–11: Learning self-control

This session is about making constructive use of anger.

Preparation

Prepare to tell a personal story from your youth about losing your temper. If you are planning to run the additional challenge, you will need pencils and paper.

Introduction

Set pupils the task of standing on one foot without wobbling for one minute. Anyone who wobbles should sit down and become an extra 'judge'. Afterwards, ask successful pupils how they did it well. Repeat, with the challenge of doing it better. Explain that controlling the movements of our bodies only comes through practice, which is why athletes train hard. Practice makes our muscles stronger and teaches our brains to control our muscles more closely. We only learned to walk with practice.

Additional challenge

Ask pupils, in pairs, to set up this target game in a spare part of the classroom. On a piece of A4 paper, draw three concentric circles with scores of 3 (in the middle), 2 and 1. Lay the target on the floor.

The object of the game is to stand close to the paper and take turns to drop (not throw) a pencil from chest height down, as near to the centre of the target as possible. Partners have five turns each, then add up the score.

Discuss in pairs, then feed back. Which parts of the body did they have to control to do this challenge well? Mention hand–eye coordination and the need to stand still when aiming. Who found that they improved after a few shots? Why do they think that was? (Our brains quickly learn how to handle an unfamiliar situation.)

Explain that we need to concentrate and practise if we want to get better at anything in school. That's why we practise skills like learning our tables.

Development

Tell a story of a time when you were young and you got into trouble by losing your temper or getting overexcited.

Explain that something like this can also happen when people play games or do something else they care about. It starts when someone gets a bit excited about something; then they get more and more excited and don't know how to stop. Something gets broken or someone gets hurt and it all ends in tears. Can pupils think of times when this has happened to them? Why? Discuss, then feed back.

Say that it's OK to be angry but it's not OK to let our anger hurt other people—saying nasty things or breaking property—or ourselves. Anger is a feeling that says, 'Something's wrong!' Of course, we could be wrong about that, too, but anger can give us the courage to make things better. (Ask your pupils to suggest some possible examples.) It might help us to do the right thing, but first we have to control it, like controlling a dog on a lead to stop it going wild.

Part of growing up is learning to take responsibility for our temper and not letting it burst out and make a situation worse. Learning to talk about our anger is a good first step towards controlling it. It's just like learning to control our other muscles. Ask, 'I wonder, what might make you cross today, and what could you do to control the feeling?'

∞ Prayer ∞

Ask everybody to shut their eyes, think of something they get cross about and imagine holding it tight in their fists. Then pray.

Father God, I get angry sometimes. Help me to talk about it and share it so that it doesn't make things worse. Help me to control my temper so that things get better.

Ask everyone to turn their hands up and gently open them, imagining the things they are cross about floating up and away. Then all say, 'Amen.'

• Thought for today •

Next time you get cross, count silently to ten, then ask yourself, 'What's really going on here?'

Unit 6

The joy of work

Background for teachers

The psychology of work can be a complex subject for schools. Although youngsters need to be prepared for the world of employment, most schools aren't obviously in the business of making a profit. That's why children and young people need to be given as many chances as possible to experience the culture of 'working life' beyond the school gates, to see what's on offer and also to understand how their class work can help them in future, if they put their minds to it.

Like many others, Christians believe that paid or unpaid work is vital for a full human life, providing us with both a personal sense of purpose and a wider social function. It's about making the most of our talents, offering something that adds value to what other people are doing or needing. Although money makes it possible to profit from sharing someone's time, skills, talents and personal energy, it can't be the only thing that matters when we go job-hunting if we want a career that develops into new opportunities and challenges. There are also dangers in defining ourselves simply in terms of what we 'do', as anyone will tell you who's been unemployed, long-term sick or newly retired. For all its importance to us, our ability to work cannot be our sole reason and justification for being here.

Story: So why do you want this job?

This is a story about a job interview. Ask pupils if they know what happens when people apply for a job. Explain that just about everybody in the room will face a job interview in their lives and it is important to prepare well for them. Can you work out what job this person is being interviewed for?

'So, Razia, why do you want this job, then?'

The manager had asked Razia the question. It comes up in every job interview. The manager wants to know if you mean what you say. You need to have a good answer ready, and it has to be the truth. A good answer is one that's got more in it than just words. It has to have you in it as well.

Razia was ready. She'd practised her own good answer several times, tried it out on friends and family, listened to their comments afterwards and adjusted it. She took a deep breath…

'I want this job because I like working with people, and this job's full of people. I'll be dealing with customers, making them feel good about what they're buying, so they'll come back next time. I'll be working alongside other staff, and I want to be part of a team. And I like the things this shop sells. They're good products at a good price. They're worth the money. Since this shop opened, I think it's brightened up the high street and made it a better place to walk along. The window displays are interesting, they're eye-catching and they get changed regularly. I reckon I could learn a lot here about working in a good shop.'

The manager nodded, looking impressed. 'That was a good answer.' Razia smiled in relief.

Then the manager looked at the notes on his desk. 'It says here that you haven't had a paid job before. Would you mind telling me why?'

This was the all-important second question, when you're asked to talk about your life before, and how you've got to this point. Razia had thought very hard about it. Her life hadn't been easy. This question was all about telling a story—not a false story, not a fairy story, but the truth, as she saw it happening. How had she got to this point? Which parts of her life had prepared her for this moment? Razia knew that, for the second question, it would take too long to talk about everything, so she should just mention the few important things. She'd practised this one, too, so she began…

'I left school without any qualifications. It was my own fault, my own mess. I didn't see the point of it all. After that, I made a lot of mistakes and bad choices that I'm just sorting out now. But one good thing happened. I had twin babies, and raising them has been the best thing I ever did. They needed all my time, but now they're ready for senior school, and they're lovely girls. When they started going to primary school, I started looking around and decided to work in a charity shop, the one I've given as a reference. I was frightened. I'd never really worked before, and the first time I was put on the till it was terrifying. But, actually, I found I could do it rather well. I liked talking to customers. I liked organising the goods on display. When the manager took a week's holiday after a few months, she put me in charge—and nothing went wrong. I was enjoying myself. I didn't realise you could enjoy working!

'So after working in that shop for three years, I think I'm ready to do this kind of thing full time and get paid for it. I've had enough of living on benefits. I want to pay my own way now. I'm ready and I want to be given a chance to show what I can do.'

She stopped. Would it work as an answer?

For a moment, there was a long silence in the room, with the background sounds of traffic moving outside in the high street, people talking as they shopped, people making a living, people like her, people wanting to get on. Her heart was racing. 'Slow down and breathe deeply,' her mum had said. 'Try not to panic. You've done your best. It's not up to you now. If you don't get this one, there'll be others.' But Razia really wanted this job.

The manager raised his eyebrows, nodded again, then spoke. 'Can you start Monday?'

Reproduced with permission from *Valuing Money* by Chris Hudson (Barnabas in Schools, 2015) www.barnabasinschools.org.uk

Religious Education

Age 5–7: Proverbs about work

The 'Wisdom' books of the Bible might be 3000 years old but some advice doesn't go out of date. The book of Proverbs is packed with shrewd observations and advice about a wide range of matters, including attitudes to work. Biblical proverbs are short, pithy nuggets of wisdom, often containing two statements, the second reinforcing or contrasting with the first. (Many translations use the wonderful old word 'sluggard' to describe a lazy person.) Examples include:

> Hardworking farmers have more than enough food; daydreamers are nothing more than stupid fools.
>
> PROVERBS 12:11

> Hard work is worthwhile, but empty talk will make you poor.
>
> PROVERBS 14:23

> The sluggard does not plough in the autumn; he will seek at harvest and have nothing.
>
> PROVERBS 20:4 (ESV)

> If you sleep all the time, you will starve; if you get up and work, you will have enough food.
>
> PROVERBS 20:13

See also Proverbs 10:3–4; 16:3; 13:4; 18:9; 21:25; 28:19.

In pairs, discuss the meaning of the proverbs. Do the pupils agree with them? Are they always true? Can people think of any real-life situations that could be examples of what these proverbs say?

Set the task of quickly copying and illustrating their favourite proverb. Then set the challenge of reading either of the classic passages below.

Bible link: Proverbs 6:6–11

> You lazy people can learn by watching an anthill.
> Ants don't have leaders,
> but they store up food during harvest season.
> How long will you lie there doing nothing at all?
> When are you going to get up and stop sleeping?
> Sleep a little. Doze a little.
> Fold your hands and twiddle your thumbs.
> Suddenly, everything is gone,
> as though it had been taken by an armed robber.

Bible link: Proverbs 24:30–34

> I once walked by the field and the vineyard of a lazy fool.
> Thorns and weeds were everywhere,
> and the stone wall had fallen down.

When I saw this, it taught me a lesson:
Sleep a little. Doze a little.
Fold your hands and twiddle your thumbs.
Suddenly poverty hits you and everything is gone!

Pupils should work in pairs to learn portions of the text by heart and prepare a short performance, adding emphasis and gestures to key words and phrases. As preparation, they could mark up enlarged copies of the text with highlighter pens.

Age 7–11: What are we here to do?

Through the centuries, philosophers and theologians have pondered the meaning of human existence, particularly in relation to the world of work. What are we doing and why are we doing it? Answering these questions helps us to keep focused and aiming for the things that really matter.

Select a National Curriculum area of knowledge or skills that the pupils have been working on lately, with obvious applications for their future working lives (for example, writing instructions, calculating with money, map work or learning a modern foreign language). In discussion, recap on the reasons why this ability might be useful for them in future, even if developing technology might make it apparently 'easier'.

Explain that all these skills help us tackle the big question of how we will work in future, but not why. People need to know why they have to do things like work—and, if they don't think about it, then they're using someone else's answers instead of their own.

Set pupils the task of discussing, then writing their answers to the question, 'What should we do when we leave school (or college)?' Feed back answers, categorising the different ambitions as necessary (for example, 'earn money', 'raise a family', 'have a place to live', 'have fun' and so on).

Ask, 'Is doing all these things the only reason we're here?' Explain that, for centuries, many people have thought hard about this—including the question, 'Is there a reason for being here at all?'

Christians have answered it by saying that people are here on this planet to help God be creative, by being creative themselves. Everything Christians do or say can be part of that creativity. For Christians, 'work' isn't just a way to make money, help others or make themselves feel good. It's a way to worship God, which ties all these things together—and that includes the work we do in school, too.

Set pupils the task of copying and illustrating one or more of the following Bible verses, explaining why the idea in it is important for Christians and then adding their own opinion.

Do your work willingly, as though you were serving the Lord himself, and not just your earthly master.

COLOSSIANS 3:23

When you eat or drink or do anything else, always do it to honour God.

1 CORINTHIANS 10:31

'Make your light shine, so that others will see the good that you do and will praise your Father in heaven.'

MATTHEW 5:16

Music

Age 7–11

'Ska' is a Jamaican dance music that came to the UK in the 1960s and goes through a revival every few years. The musician known as Prince Buster produced his own ska version of the song 'Enjoy yourself', adding lyrics containing a positive message for children and young people about using their school years to maximise their skills and talents. Display the lyrics from www.allmusic.com/song/enjoy-yourself-mt0013630381/lyrics and play pupils a performance of them, sourced from YouTube or elsewhere.

Read and discuss the lyrics in the verses. What does Prince Buster really mean when he tells people, 'Enjoy yourself'?

Together, experiment with creating the steady '1–2 1–2' beat, placing the emphasis on the first half of the beat, adding percussion as necessary but especially singing the words 'with a swing', adding emphasis and gestures to amplify the message. You could prepare a performance for an assembly.

Ask pupils to reflect on what it might really mean to 'enjoy yourself' in the fullest sense, creating acrostic poetry on that theme.

Circle Time

Age 5–11: Discovering my talents

This session explores how 'talent' is something that has to be worked at.

Preparation

Practise demonstrating a personal skill you enjoy, such as juggling, playing a musical instrument, knitting, drawing, mental maths, writing a poem dramatically or telling a funny story.

Introduction

Demonstrate your personal skill. Tell the story of how you first learned it, describing the pitfalls and difficulties, and say who helped you to improve. Say what you like about doing it.

Development

Ask, 'If we say somebody is genuinely talented, what does that mean?' Ask for and list the names of some famous people with the headings 'Famous people' and 'Talented at what?' on the board. Try to include people with a range of talents from broad areas of society: sport and light entertainment are fine for starters, but also mention the fields of art, literature, music of all kinds, technology, construction and engineering, business, science, health and medicine, education, politics, the church and other areas of faith and belief.

Explain that although everybody is born with a range of talents, we don't naturally get better at them unless we persevere. Somebody once said, 'Being a genius is ten per cent inspiration and 90 per cent perspiration.' We have to practise our skills and learn new ones from other people who are already good at them. Real enjoyment requires effort, unlike 'having fun', which is instant and easy. Every famous person who has mastered a set of skills will tell you that having a talent is only the first step. Making the most of yourself means having to say, 'I'm going to get better at this' and working at it, day after day, week after week.

Encourage pupils to think about the skills and talents that they all have. With partners, discuss what you think each person is good at, and feed back. Are there any surprises? (Flag up social skills, which are always worth encouraging.) How might the class improve those talents and abilities? One day, would some of them enable pupils to help others or build a family and a career?

∞ Prayer ∞

Father God, you made me with a whole range of skills and talents, some of which I don't even know about yet. Help me find out what they are, and give me the courage to work at them when life is tough. Show me how to use them, one day, to serve others and make your world a better place. Amen

· Thought for today ·

What are my hidden talents?

Unit 7

Speculation and investment

Background for teachers

There's money in flowers. 'Tulipomania' was the name given to a wave of financial speculation in the Netherlands during the 1630s, as millions of florins were invested in the collection and production of rare tulip bulbs. Many people were trying to make money from buying bulbs that were bound to increase in value, to be sold on at a profit… or so they thought. Of course, it all went wrong, and some rich speculators were left with very expensive flowerbeds that looked good but weren't worth very much. Some historians and economists now wonder if the story has been exaggerated, but, when other modern investment scandals (such as 'Bitcoins') are discussed, Tulipomania is often mentioned too.

Pupils might find the following story funny, but it's surprising how our sense of 'value' can lead us into parting with large sums of money for items that may not, in themselves, be worth very much. Children are particularly prone to the natural urge to build up collections of favourite things (trading cards, model figures, stickers and so on), especially if everyone else in the playground is seen to be doing it. (See the assembly script 'Don't be fooled!' on page 98.) Many children and adults get sucked into the notion that their collectables will be worth something some day. They probably won't—but the sellers may be!

Story: Tulips from Amsterdam

The Amsterdam courtroom was packed and the judge impatient. 'Send the prisoner in!' he commanded.

A guard strode out, returning shortly with his hand on the shoulder of a nervous man wearing handcuffs. The prisoner looked rather frightened. All these angry people were staring at him. What was he doing here? It was all an accident. He had just made a silly mistake. Anyone could have done it. Why had they locked him up in the town jail? Now he was standing in the dock to hear the charges. His name and occupation were read out to the court by a lawyer—'Albert Tripp, English sailor'—and then the judge spoke.

'The charge is this—that you willingly stole and destroyed a valuable item belonging to Mr Geert Langsgaard, a merchant in our town. At his counting-house, you took this valuable item from his desk, placed it in your pocket and then later destroyed it.'

Albert's face was pale. 'Umm… can I explain?'

'Do you plead guilty or not guilty?'

'I thought it was an onion.'

'I repeat, do you plead guilty or not guilty?'

'It was a mistake! I didn't know!'

The judge sighed. 'That is not the point. But if you plead guilty, any explanation you then give might lead to a lighter sentence, if we are sympathetic. So how do you plead?'

A long pause. 'Guilty. But I'm sorry!'

The judge let out another long breath. 'Well, then. Tell your story.'

After promising to tell only the truth, the whole truth and nothing but the truth (so help him God), the sailor told his tale.

'I was at the counting-house because Mr Langsgaard had said he wanted to know, as soon as possible, that our ship had arrived. So, when we docked, I was sent to tell him we were here and ready to unload. He was really pleased: he shook my hand and offered to buy me some breakfast. One of his servants brought me some nice pickled herring to eat and left me in the office. Now I've had pickled herring before—it's how you eat fish in Amsterdam—but there wasn't any chopped onion to go with it. You've got to have chopped onion with your herring. I looked around and there was an onion sitting on a desk. So I took it.'

There was a sigh around the courtroom.

'I went back to the docks, bought a bread roll, sat down on a bench, took out my knife and had my breakfast. I cut up the herring, sliced up the onion and put them in the roll. And I ate them. That's all I did!'

People groaned. The judge raised his hand. 'You thought Mr Langsgaard's tulip bulb was an onion?'

'Yes.'

The judge winced. 'How did it taste?'

'Not good, but I was hungry.' There was another groan around the courtroom.

Reproduced with permission from *Valuing Money* by Chris Hudson (Barnabas in Schools, 2015) www.barnabasinschools.org.uk

'Mister Tripp, did you know that some tulip bulbs in this country are being sold for a great deal of money?'

'I do now, my Lord.'

'But do you know how much this one cost? It was a Semper Augustus, costing 3000 florins. In case you do not understand our Dutch currency, let me make this clear. Your breakfast cost Mr Langsgaard enough money to pay for a complete royal banquet, or it would feed your English ship's crew for a whole year. Do you understand now? That bulb was an investment. Unless you can pay him back, I must sentence you to six months in our town jail. Do you have anything to say?'

'Er… no. I'm only a sailor. I haven't got that sort of money. Why did he leave it just lying around like that? Can't I pay him back bit by bit?'

The judge looked at Mr Langsgaard, who furiously shook his head, then turned back.

'No. I sentence you to six months in jail. Do you have anything else to say?'

'Yes. I hope the breakfasts in jail taste better than that bulb!'

Explain that this court case really happened in the Netherlands, 300 years ago. For a time, some rare tulip bulbs became more expensive than jewellery, simply because they were rare. But bulbs can be used to make more bulbs (you can't do that with jewellery), which means that, at some point, your rare bulbs stop being rare and then they lose their value. People can still be fooled by thoughts of making a lot of money very quickly and it can all go wrong.

Reproduced with permission from *Valuing Money* by Chris Hudson (Barnabas in Schools, 2015) www.barnabasinschools.org.uk

Religious Education

Age 5–7: The love of money

Ask, 'Who here would like to be rich? If you could have a lot of money, what would you do with it?' Some people have thought that the Christian Bible says, 'Money is the root of all evil', but that's not true. In 1 Timothy 6:10, the apostle Paul writes, 'The love of money causes all kinds of trouble. Some people want money so much that they have given up their faith and caused themselves a lot of pain.'

On the other hand, the author Mark Twain said, 'Lack of money is the root of all evil.'

What do your pupils think is the most dangerous thing in the world—wanting money or not having enough money? Discuss these two ideas. Is there any way they could both be dangerous?

Set the task of drawing somebody who has just found a £20 note lying on the ground and, in thought bubbles, showing what this person might be thinking. If they were a Christian who took Paul's words seriously, what might they do with the money? What would your class do?

Age 7–11: Parables about 'true treasure'

Share these parables of Jesus with the class. He said that the kingdom of God is like a man who discovered treasure in a neighbour's field and decided that the only legal way of getting his hands on it was by selling everything he had to buy the field. He also said that it was like a jewellery expert who sacrificed all his other jewels to acquire the greatest one of all.

Bible link: Matthew 13:44–46

The kingdom of heaven is like what happens when someone finds a treasure hidden in a field and buries it again. A person like that is happy and goes and sells everything in order to buy that field.

The kingdom of heaven is like what happens when a shop owner is looking for fine pearls. After finding a very valuable one, the owner goes and sells everything in order to buy that pearl.

What do your pupils think is the key message of these parables? (There is a cost to being part of God's kingdom. Sometimes you have to be ready to 'sacrifice', to lose things that aren't so important, to get your hands on the things that are really important.)

Share the following words, which Jesus spoke about 'treasure'.

Bible link: Luke 12:33–34; Matthew 6:19–21

Sell what you have and give the money to the poor. Make yourselves moneybags that never wear out. Make sure your treasure is safe in heaven, where thieves cannot steal it and moths cannot destroy it. Your heart will always be where your treasure is.

Don't store up treasures on earth! Moths and rust can destroy them, and thieves can break in and steal them. Instead, store up your treasures in heaven, where moths and rust cannot destroy them, and thieves cannot break in and steal them. Your heart will always be where your treasure is.

Ask, 'What do we think are the key life messages here? What are your own life ambitions? What would you want your life to be like when you are 16, 18, 25, 40, 50 or 60?'

Set the task of constructing a personal illustrated timeline for the future, including the fulfilment of three important ambitions.

Discuss

• Do you think a Christian who took Jesus' words seriously would have these same ambitions? Why? Why not?

• What might a Christian's 'treasure' be?

What's your treasure? Children will be familiar with the idea of school crazes where suddenly everybody has to have the latest gadget, fashion item or set of collectables. Marketing experts know how to play on this desire, which is why so much advertising shows other people apparently enjoying a product. It's saying, 'If you buy this, it will make your life so much better—look at these people enjoying it!' Deconstructing these messages helps children to see what is really going on.

Age 5–7: Branded packaging

'Brand recognition' of products began in the Victorian age as suppliers of goods realised that purchasers wanted to be able to trust that the thing they were buying was of a consistently good quality. Packaging rapidly became stylised as producers established their products in the minds of the public with clear brand names, colours, fonts, logos, images and catchphrases.

Prepare by obtaining a large cereal packet that's been designed to appeal to children. Introduce the lesson by mentioning how advertisers try to give packaging 'pester-power', using all sorts of clever tricks to make children ask their parents to buy something in the supermarket. Then pass the packet around the class (starting with the less able pupils), asking each child to notice something different about the packaging, while you scribe their responses on display.

Note the different sizes of lettering, which draw attention to certain features first. Then discuss which features were especially designed to appeal to children. (You could also open out a box, photocopy all the printed sides at a reduced size, then ask pupils to study it and annotate the key features.)

Set the challenge of creating the front of a new box of horrible cereal that the makers are desperate to sell to children. ('Yummy Bunny Droppings?')

Extension

Show examples of how one product has been packaged differently over the decades. What changes do the pupils notice?

Age 7–11: TV adverts—Lights, camera, action

Prepare up to three recordings of age-appropriate broadcast commercials designed to appeal to children, especially ones featuring child actors.

Explain that, unlike other types of TV programming, adverts are designed to sell things to people. Everything we see or hear happening in a commercial is there to make us buy something. If we see someone who looks or sounds like us, enjoying a product, that's because the makers want us to identify with that experience.

Show at least one of the adverts twice. On the second showing, assign groups of pupils the task of discussing and noting down some of the following features:

- The key features of the product that the makers want you to remember
- The key expressions and responses of the child actors
- Words, phrases, images, text, music and dramatic events used to reinforce their message
- Pupils' own feelings about the advert. On a scale of 1–10, how strongly do they think the advert made them want to buy the product? Why did it have that impact?

Groups can feed back their responses for general class discussion. Individuals should then write a report about the advert, describing its key messages and how they were reinforced.

Extension

Set the task of scripting an advert, using the same techniques, to try to either sell an unlikely spoof product or persuade people to give money regularly to a real charity.

Drama

Age 7–11: 'Halt! Hand over your tulips!'

On YouTube, find and show the classic 1970s Monty Python sketch 'Dennis Moore', in which a highwayman holds up a stagecoach to demand that the passengers hand over their cargo of lupin flowers, then redistributes them to the baffled local poor.

Warm up by practising facial expressions and gestures for terror, outrage, greed and so on.

Set groups of pupils the challenge of recreating the dialogue for the scene—only this time the stagecoach is carrying a cargo of 'precious' tulip bulbs. Every member of each team has to contribute something to the hammed-up dialogue, which should last about a minute. ('No! Not my precious bulbs!' 'You'll never get away with this!') If there is time, add gestures and simple movements.

Circle Time

Age 5–11: Love, the ultimate treasure?

This session explores the importance of love in our growth as people.

Preparation

You will need a picture of a baby.

Introduction

Display your picture of a baby. Ask, 'Who here has had a baby in the house? What's it like? How does having a baby change the way you have to live?' Pupils can share their experiences.

Development

Say, 'We've been thinking about treasure. Here's somebody's little treasure!' (Show picture.)

Explain that babies are born with all sorts of needs. Ask pupils to discuss, in pairs, the question, 'What does a baby need to be happy and comfortable?' Feed back, listing the obvious issues like warmth and milk for nutrition, but also the crucial need for affection from others: a baby needs to know that it is loved. Ask, 'How would a baby know this?' Take answers and list them on the board, adding the following if they are not mentioned: kisses and cuddles, gazing into eyes, talking and stroking. Explain that this is how babies learn to trust others: they learn that they are valued, by having all their needs met, time and time again.

When we're born, we're all at the centre of our own little world. In a way, you could say we are all born selfish—but then we start growing up and we realise that other people have needs as well. They need to be loved, too. The sooner we realise this, the more grown-up we are. Maturity isn't about simply getting older in years; it's about learning how to love others, and it takes a lifetime to get right.

In the Christian Bible, Paul writes this:

> Love is kind and patient, never jealous, boastful, proud, or rude. Love isn't selfish or quick tempered. It doesn't keep a record of wrongs that others do. Love rejoices in the truth, but not in evil. Love is always supportive, loyal, hopeful, and trusting. Love never fails!
>
> 1 CORINTHIANS 13:4–8

Could this kind of love be a 'treasure'?

∞ Prayer ∞

Father God, help me to learn how to love others. Help me to seek the greatest treasure of all. Amen

· Thought for today ·

What's your treasure?

Unit 8

Valuing people

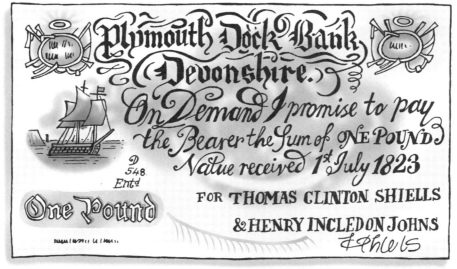

Background for teachers

What is a human being actually worth? For Olaudah Equiano, the answer was 'Forty pounds'. In 1766, that's the amount of money he'd saved to buy his freedom on the West Indian island of Montserrat. Enslaved as a child, he'd been sold from owner to owner until he learnt the lucrative skills of reading, writing and business accountancy. As a street trader (away from his normal work), Olaudah saved enough cash to purchase his freedom from his owner, which he then used to travel and campaign against the horrors of slavery. His autobiography *The Interesting Narrative* sold out many editions in his lifetime and still provides fascinating glimpses of the slave trade, told from the inside by a subversive survivor.

There's money to be made from treating vulnerable people as things to be bought and sold, and setting a 'price' on someone has consequences for the way they are then treated. The Atlantic Slave Trade generated immense amounts of wealth for Great Britain, financing much of the Industrial Revolution that forged a great world power. Despite this, most British people never saw slavery's worst excesses because it was forbidden on British soil (although practising it in foreign parts was considered acceptable). It took decades of campaigning from the likes of Olaudah Equiano, Thomas Clarkson, William Wilberforce and Hannah More to convince the public that Britain didn't need the profits of slavery to be truly 'Great'. Despite official abolition in a wide range of countries, slavery continues to exist in today's world in a variety of guises. Who makes your clothes?

When discussing the slave trade, always be careful to consider the feelings of pupils who may have historic family connections with slavery and be alert to any expressions of prejudice, conscious or otherwise. This unit of work explains how many of our racial prejudices have economic roots based on old injustices.

Story: **Wings on his feet**

He was flying. That's what it felt like, dashing along the streets towards the Register Office to buy his freedom. It felt as if his feet had wings. Olaudah had saved up enough money to buy his freedom and now it was finally happening. No more being a slave! No more being somebody else's property! 'FREE! AT LAST! THANK YOU, GOD!'

Would the office be open? It had to be open today, on this day of all days. Please, God, don't let it be shut. This moment had been so long coming. Olaudah had been slowly saving his cash, buying and selling a few things here and there as he sailed around the Caribbean from port to port, serving his rich owner. He would perhaps see some glass tumblers and a jug for sale cheap in one marketplace, then buy and sell them on for more money in another. Bit by bit, his savings had grown.

Then it happened. He finally had enough money to buy his freedom. With the ship's captain, Olaudah went to see his master, Robert King, in his office, carrying £40 in large used notes. In 1766, that was a lot of cash. Nervously, they knocked on the boss's door, heard a 'Yes?' and went in. Robert King was sitting at a desk by the window, checking figures in an account book. 'Well, what do you want?' he said, without looking up.

A moment's silence, then Olaudah reached in his pocket to produce the notes and quietly laid £40 down on the desk in front of him.

'What?' Robert King looked up, frowning.

'That's to buy my freedom, sir. As we agreed.'

King picked up the notes and counted them, putting them down suspiciously. 'Forty pounds? Where did you get it?'

'Honestly, sir.' Olaudah's face was blank. From long, painful experience, he knew the rules with owners and masters. Don't make him cross. Don't give him the excuse to change his mind.

King scowled. 'I made that promise two years ago. If I'd known you could make it that quickly, I wouldn't have promised,' he snorted. 'You make money faster than I do!'

Olaudah's friend intervened. 'Oh, come on, Robert! You promised him while I was there, and he's kept his side of the bargain. He made all that money above board, and he'll still make money for you as a free man… won't you, Gustavus?'

Olaudah nodded vigorously. Gustavus was his slave name, the one they'd given him. Yes. He would promise to carry on working for now. He'd promise almost anything. But just say 'yes', he pleaded silently. I want my freedom. Say 'yes'. Now. Please God, make him say 'yes'.

Robert King sighed and placed his hand on the £40 again. 'Well, I'm a man who keeps his promises. I'll be as good as my word.' Extracting a large pocketwatch on a chain from his waistcoat, he checked the time. 'Listen, the Register Office closes at five o'clock. Tell the Register I want a manumission letter drawn up. Manumission, got that? It'll cost you a guinea, mind, not me. Understand? Bring that letter back and I'll sign it. Off you go, then… Gustavus, did you hear me?'

Then Olaudah realised. Yes. Robert King had said 'yes'. Tears came to his eyes, he bowed, said 'thank you' many times, politely shook the hands of Robert and the captain, turned and left the room. Then, as soon as he was outside, he punched the air—and ran. With wings on his feet.

Reproduced with permission from *Valuing Money* by Chris Hudson (Barnabas in Schools, 2015) www.barnabasinschools.org.uk

He was nearly there now. The Register Office was open and the man in charge was surprisingly friendly. 'Well done, lad! We don't see too many of these, so I'll let you have it at half price.' Soon, the letter was written, the money handed over, and Olaudah was dashing back along the streets, clutching that precious piece of paper with his freedom written all over it.

'So, Gustavus,' asked Robert King, when he had the letter in his hands, 'you will carry on working for me, won't you? I need someone reliable on my ship to keep an eye on the money. And this time, you'll be paid.'

Olaudah nodded. Then King took his pen and wrote his name at the bottom of the letter. The captain signed it, too, as a legal witness, clapped his hands and they all shook hands, like friends. 'I'm a free man,' thought Olaudah. It was all going to change now. He had a dream of finding a place to live where no one could ever make him a slave again. It was a place he'd heard about where everyone was equal, and 'the air was too pure to allow slavery'. That's what a High Court judge had said. England. One day, he would live there. He'd carry on working for Robert King just for now, but England was calling him. Once he was living there as a free man, Olaudah would tell them all the truth about slavery—and one day, it would be stopped.

After telling the story, ask, 'Do you think it was right that Olaudah had to buy his freedom at all? What other questions do you have about this story?'

In discussion, point out how Olaudah had been given a 'slave name', which he stopped using as soon as possible. He finally made England his home, where he married and raised a family, between making more voyages around the world as a paid-up member of a ship's crew. He also wrote a bestselling autobiography that opened many people's eyes to the evils of slavery.

Reproduced with permission from *Valuing Money* by Chris Hudson (Barnabas in Schools, 2015) www.barnabasinschools.org.uk

Religious Education

Over the next few years, after buying his freedom, Olaudah became a Christian. When he started campaigning against the slave trade, he declared that it was wrong for Christians to buy and sell human beings, because everyone was equally special to God, who had no favourites.

Age 5–7: Treating people as people

Ask pupils to act out some of the jobs that slaves had to do in the West Indies during Olaudah's time, such as cutting down large stalks of sugar cane with a sharp heavy knife, stirring boiling sugar syrup in a steaming vat, cleaning around the house, sweeping the ground and carrying heavy rocks. Explain that, nowadays, farmers would have to pay someone to do this kind of work, but slaves didn't get paid. A slave just had to do the work, day after day.

Seat the class in two circles, one circle inside the other, as slaves and owners. The owners then decide what hard work the slaves should be doing. What body language would the owners be showing as their slaves were working? What would they be shouting, telling the slaves to do?

Act this scenario out for a minute, with both groups in role, then swap over roles and repeat.

Discuss how it would feel to be an owner or a slave. Brainstorm words describing these feelings, asking for reasons as well.

Olaudah clearly didn't like being treated as a piece of property. Do your pupils think slavery was fair or unfair to the slaves? What would have made it more fair? Explain that most people now think that slavery is definitely wrong. In the Christian Bible, Paul writes that God doesn't see some people as being more important than others, like slaves and free people, or even men and women or boys and girls. When we become friends of Jesus, then we are all in the same family—God's family (see Galatians 3:28).

Ask every child to draw or colour in a named picture of themselves for display, with the caption 'Christians believe that everybody is important to God'.

Extension

Ask pupils to write in their exercise books the heading 'Slavery is about treating people as property.'

Discuss this idea, then list a few of the most powerful words the class can think of, describing 'feelings about slavery'.

Ask pupils to copy and illustrate part or all of Galatians 3:28, highlighting the most important words and phrases in their opinion, then explaining their choice.

Age 7–11: Slavery in the Bible

In the first century AD, many slaves in the Roman Empire were attracted to Christianity because it treated all believers as equal in the eyes of God. Many of them identified with the suffering of Jesus when he was arrested, because it was horribly similar to their own situation. One letter in the New Testament tells the story of Onesimus, a runaway slave who became a Christian. Paul, the author of the letter to Philemon, wanted Onesimus to be reconciled to Philemon, his Christian master. Slavery isn't being directly challenged in this letter, but we can see that Paul is urging Philemon to treat the runaway slave as a human being, not simply as 'property' with a financial value.

Explain the background to the letter, then read out the following extract.

Bible link: Philemon 1, 10–18

From Paul, who is in jail for serving Christ Jesus, and from Timothy, who is like a brother because of our faith.

Philemon, you work with us and are very dear to us…

I beg you to help Onesimus! He is like a son to me because I led him to Christ here in jail. Before this, he was useless to you, but now he is useful both to you and to me.

Sending Onesimus back to you makes me very sad. I would like to keep him here with me, where he could take your place in helping me while I am here in prison for preaching the good news. But I won't do anything unless you agree to it first. I want your act of kindness to come from your heart, and not be something you feel forced to do.

Perhaps Onesimus was taken from you for a little while so that you could have him back for good, but not as a slave. Onesimus is much more than a slave. To me he is a dear friend, but to you he is even more, both as a person and as a follower of the Lord.

If you consider me a friend because of Christ, then welcome Onesimus as you would welcome me. If he has cheated you or owes you anything, charge it to my account.

Discuss the questions 'What is Paul saying? What does he want Philemon to do?'

See www.barnabasinschools.org.uk/friendship-breakup for suggestions of ways to follow up this activity in drama or discussion.

Extensions

Olaudah Equiano often used Bible texts to underline his campaign against slavery. To explore this further, visit 'Opening Up the King James Bible', a free teacher resource on the Barnabas in Schools website, which includes detailed lesson plans about the war of ideas concerning the Atlantic slave trade in the 18th century. See www.barnabasinschools.org.uk/openingupthekingjamesbible/

As a literacy extension, ask pupils to analyse Paul's letter to Philemon as an exercise in persuasive writing.

Numeracy

Age 9–11

Exchange rates for different currencies can go up or down, and we have to be careful to remember what our own money is worth when we exchange and spend it abroad. In 1766, Olaudah Equiano's £40 was worth a great deal more than it is today, and it took him two years of extra work to save it all up.

Ask pupils to research what that £40 would be worth today. Do they think that should be the 'price' of a human being? As a rough classroom guide, £1 in 1766 would be worth nearly £200 today. The Bank of England has a useful historical inflation calculator available online at:

www.bankofengland.co.uk/education/pages/resources/inflationtools/calculator/index1.aspx

In 1766, there were 240 pennies to a pre-decimalised pound. Because the money was worth more than it is today, they had smaller fractions of a penny, such as halfpennies and farthings (quarter pennies) to use in everyday buying and selling. A penny would be worth too much for smaller transactions.

This is how some everyday items were valued in London at the time when Olaudah was buying his freedom in Montserrat. (A penny was written as 1d.)

- $\frac{1}{2}$d (half a penny) = half a loaf of bread or a glass of gin.
- 1d (one penny) = a loaf of bread, one pint of beer, two glasses of gin or a day's heating for one person (in coal).
- 1$\frac{1}{2}$d (one and a half pence) = a pound (454g) of soap or the hourly pay for a boy to chop firewood.
- 2d (tuppence) = four glasses of gin.
- 3d (thruppence) = a supper of bread, cheese and beer or the cost of posting a one-page letter.
- 4d (fourpence) = a quart (two pints) of beer or a boat ride across the River Thames.

Ask the class to find out the approximate costs for some of these products or services today, and compare them to the 1766 prices, multiplied by 200. Who do you think was paying more or less for them—people in 1766 or people today?

Can pupils think of any other interesting questions about this price list? How might the values affect what people were buying, and what effect might this have had? For example, what could happen in a world where alcoholic drinks like gin were as cheap as normal food? How would drinking lots of gin affect a family's lifestyle and general health? Remember that children were allowed to buy alcoholic drinks too—and alcohol is more dangerous for children than it is for adults.

Circle Time

Age 5–11: Will you be my friend?

This session is about how prejudice affects people.

Across Europe, the Atlantic slave trade encouraged an assumption that white people were superior to those with darker skins. This idea was reinforced by European empire-building in the 19th century and early-20th century 'scientific' ideas about race.

Preparation

You will need blue and green stickers or badges.

Introduction

You could run the classic role-play lesson that exists in several versions, in which pupils are randomly allocated blue or green badges or stickers and the two groups are made to sit separately in the room. For a short time, the teacher treats the groups differently as they perform a lesson activity such as completing a series of number problems. (One group could be given harder problems and less time, and the teacher could make comments such as 'I'd expect that sort of thing from a *Blue*!')

Be sensitive to the needs of individual pupils if you choose to run this activity, and emphasise beforehand that it is role play. You don't really mean it.

Discuss the feelings we get when a simple label is used to judge people. We call this 'prejudice'.

Development

Tell the following story. You could dramatise it yourself by playing the girl, using some willing members of the class as assistants.

There was once a girl who moved to a new school, claiming that she'd been bullied at her previous school. 'Will you be my friend?' she asked all the children in her new class. All of them agreed, but then her teacher noticed some strange things happening at playtime. The new girl kept finding fault with people. 'You're taller than me. I don't like people who are taller than me.' Then it was 'You've got long hair. I don't like people who've got long hair... You like playing football. I don't like people who like football.' Over the weeks and bit by bit, her circle of friends was getting smaller and smaller, until finally she hardly had any friends and could sometimes be seen standing at the edge of the playground, complaining. One day, her parents came in to say, 'We're moving our child to another school, as she's obviously being bullied here.'

What would your class want to say to the girl and her parents?

In discussion, draw out how the girl was noticing all the things that made people different and then judging people badly because of the differences. That's prejudice. People can be prejudiced about anything—colour of hair, colour of skin, our accent, where our parents come from, our faith or beliefs, whether we wear glasses or hearing aids or need a wheelchair, how much money we have… the list can go on and on. Sometimes, it's said that a whole bunch of people are better or worse than others. The Atlantic Slave Trade sucked in Olaudah Equiano and thousands like him, and it led many Europeans to think that people with dark skins weren't as good as people with lighter-colour skins. That's a bit like saying that having a bigger or smaller nose makes you cleverer than others!

In the Bible, Jesus tells his followers, 'Love others as much as you love yourself' (Mark 12:31). What would he have to say about anyone who judges people by the colour of their skin or whether they need glasses? Discuss in small groups, then feed back.

∞ Prayer/meditation ∞

Ask pupils to study one of their own fingers, examining the fingerprint, then comparing it to their neighbour's and noticing the differences. Explain that no one in the world has the same fingerprint as someone else, even if they are twins. No one has ever had that print before and no one ever will. We are all unique, meaning 'one of a kind'.

Father God, you made us all different. Thank you for all the things that make us unique and special. Help us to appreciate all the things in ourselves and other people that make us special and loved by you. Amen

• Thought for today •

Everybody here is a work of art. Let's learn to appreciate each other!

Unit 9

How spending affects others

Background for teachers

'Fair trade' isn't a new idea. The 18th-century campaigners for the abolition of slavery realised that customers for slave-produced goods needed to be offered ethical alternatives, so, 200 years ago, they sponsored the creation of fair trade products, long before it became as fashionable as it sometimes is today.

Thomas Clarkson's lifelong campaign against the Atlantic slave trade encouraged William Wilberforce and many others to take up the fight, both in Parliament and around the country. Olaudah Equiano (see Unit 8) was living in London by this time, and he became a key supporter, friend and source of useful information. Although Clarkson finally succeeded in getting the trade abolished in 1807 (and slavery itself within the British Empire in 1833), it still exists around the world in many forms today, when vulnerable people are exploited, living in terrible conditions for little or no wages.

The modern Fairtrade movement offers positive alternatives. Our global economy provides lots of opportunities for ethical and unethical producers to sell their goods to the richer countries, but customers can exercise a lot of power when they choose what to buy. The few extra pence we might spend on a Fairtrade product can make a lot of difference to the people who produce it. Some schools operate weekly Fairtrade tuck shops, run by the oldest children. Could that happen in your school? See http://schools.fairtrade.org.uk.

Story: Bittersweet

It was a quiet afternoon in the coffee shop when the stranger came in. He was smartly dressed and carrying a large wooden chest, which now sat on the floor beside him. He'd ordered a coffee and cake and was writing something in a notebook as they arrived on a tray.

'Sugar, sir?' asked the shopkeeper as he placed the coffee pot on the table.

'No, thanks,' said the stranger, reaching down to open the wooden chest and pull out a small bag. 'I've brought my own.'

'I beg your pardon, sir?'

'I've brought my own.'

The owner looked puzzled. 'Is it better than the sugar we have here, sir?'

'Not really. It tastes exactly the same, actually. I just prefer using this.' The stranger used a teaspoon to shovel some sugar from his bag into his coffee cup, then stirred it in.

The shopkeeper thought this a bit odd. 'Why? What's wrong with our sugar, then?'

'Well…' replied the stranger, 'it's because I know where my sugar came from. It wasn't grown and harvested by enslaved Africans in the West Indies. It's from Africa, produced by free people. Excuse me for asking, but where does your sugar come from for this shop?'

'Down the market, sir. From Mr Tate's stall.'

The stranger sighed. 'Well, I'm afraid to say that Mr Tate's sugar is produced by slaves. Do you know what goes into making sugar in Jamaica or Barbados? No? They chain people together on the ships before they leave Africa, and some of them die as they're shipped across the Atlantic. When they arrive, families are split up and sold to work for the highest bidder. Some farmers whip children to make them work harder and it's all done to make money for the farmers and sugar for our coffee tables back here in England. So… I prefer my own.' He held up the bag. 'Do you want a taste? It was produced by free people who were paid a decent wage for their work. If you like it, I could supply you with enough sugar for your shop every week. I'm sure they'd thank you for it.'

The owner scowled. 'You're that Mister Thomas Clarkson, aren't you? You're one of these Abolitionists. You've come down to Bristol from London with your fancy ideas, to tear down everything that makes our city great. The Atlantic trade has made us England's pride, and you want to smash it all to bits. Sir, I think you should leave my shop now!'

Thomas Clarkson put down his cup. 'Sir, Bristol's a fine city, but when I go down to the harbour and see the masts of all those ships, ready to sail away and carry innocent people across the Atlantic to an early death, it frightens me. One day, we'll be paying a heavy price for it.'

'OUT! NOW!'

With a sigh, Thomas picked up his wooden chest and walked out. Bang! The door was slammed shut behind him. He was used to it. Lifting the chest on to his shoulder, he strode down the street towards the Quaker meeting-house, where people were gathering to hear him speak. Inside the chest were samples of African cloth, wood, seeds, sugar, cocoa beans, coffee beans and all sorts of other goods, produced by free people earning a fair wage, not slaves.

'Look at all these wonderful things,' he was going to say. 'Beautiful things, produced by amazing people.' They could all be imported from Africa and sold here on the dockside in Bristol, if he could just find some customers. Would these Quakers listen? He didn't know—but even here, in this great city lying at the heart of the Atlantic slave trade, Thomas thought it was worth a try.

After telting the story, say that Thomas Clarkson (1760–1846) spent 48 years of his life trying to stop the African slave trade across the British Empire. He finally won, and Parliament made it illegal in 1833. His original 'African chest' can be seen on display at Wilberforce House in Kingston-upon-Hull. You can see images of it here:

historicalmovies.
files.wordpress.
com/2010/08/wil4.jpg

abolition.e2bn.org/
library/0711/0000/0049/
dscf2807mid_360.jpg

A virtual version can be found at museumbox.e2bn.
org/creator/viewer/
show/34

Reproduced with permission from Valuing Money *by Chris Hudson (Barnabas in Schools, 2015) www.barnabasinschools.org.uk*

Religious Education

Age 5–7: What's fair?

Jesus' parable of the workers in the vineyard tells how a succession of casual labourers are hired to work in a vineyard at intervals through the day until the end, when they all receive exactly the same wages from the owner (who represents God), however long they've worked. It's not a satisfactory model for industrial relations (what would happen if the owner tried it again next day?), but the vineyard owner's bottom line seems to be about getting the job done and giving every worker a basic minimum wage on which to live.

Bible link: Matthew 20:1–16

As Jesus was telling what the kingdom of heaven would be like, he said:

Early one morning a man went out to hire some workers for his vineyard. After he had agreed to pay them the usual amount for a day's work, he sent them off to his vineyard.

About nine that morning, the man saw some other people standing in the market with nothing to do. He said he would pay them what was fair, if they would work in his vineyard. So they went.

At noon and again about three in the afternoon he returned to the market. And each time he made the same agreement with others who were loafing around with nothing to do.

Finally, about five in the afternoon the man went back and found some others standing there. He asked them, 'Why have you been standing here all day long doing nothing?'

'Because no one has hired us,' they answered. Then he told them to go work in his vineyard.

That evening the owner of the vineyard told the man in charge of the workers to call them in and give them their money. He also told the man to begin with the ones who were hired last. When the workers arrived, the ones who had been hired at five in the afternoon were given a full day's pay.

The workers who had been hired first thought they would be given more than the others. But when they were given the same, they began complaining to the owner of the vineyard. They said, 'The ones who were hired last worked for only one hour. But you paid them the same that you did us. And we worked in the hot sun all day long!'

The owner answered one of them, 'Friend, I didn't cheat you. I paid you exactly what we agreed on. Take your money now and go! What business is it of yours if I want to pay them the same that I paid you? Don't I have the right to do what I want with my own money? Why should you be jealous, if I want to be generous?'

Jesus then said, 'So it is. Everyone who is now first will be last, and everyone who is last will be first.'

Retell this story through drama, with four groups of children representing the different workers being hired throughout the day. Jobs might include preparing a vineyard (gathering stones, ploughing, weeding, spreading manure, planting) or harvesting. Have one child playing the vineyard owner, who promises each group a fair wage when they're hired. When it's the time to stop work, call each group up to be 'paid', starting with the first, then tell them to watch closely as the owner pays everyone exactly the same.

What is the first group's reaction to the later workers being paid the same? The last group had been trying to get hired all day, and failing. What might they be thinking?

Discuss the following questions. What message does this story give about God's view of what's fair in our world? According to the story, what might God want for everybody?

Ask pupils to copy Jesus' final words in the story—'Everyone who is now first will be last, and everyone who is last will be first'—and then write or illustrate what they think 'fairness' means. What might fairness mean for the way we spend our money today?

Age 7–11: Fair trade and treasure

As part of his famous Sermon on the Mount, Jesus told his followers to beware of chasing after things that weren't really important, such as tasting the finest food or wearing the most expensive clothes. In his opinion, setting one's heart on blindly following the latest fashions in food or clothes wasn't worth the trouble. Instead, he offered something more—the opportunity to be citizens in the 'kingdom of God' with assets that couldn't wear out, rot away or be stolen.

Bible link: Luke 12:22–34

Jesus said to his disciples:

I tell you not to worry about your life! Don't worry about having something to eat or wear. Life is more than food or clothing. Look at the crows! They don't plant or harvest, and they don't have storehouses or barns. But God takes care of them. You are much more important than any birds. Can worry make you live longer? If you don't have power over small things, why worry about everything else?

Look how the wild flowers grow! They don't work hard to make their clothes. But I tell you that Solomon with all his wealth wasn't as well clothed as one of these flowers. God gives such beauty to everything that grows in the fields, even though it is here today and thrown into a fire tomorrow. Won't he do even more for you? You have such little faith!

Don't keep worrying about having something to eat or drink. Only people who don't know God are always worrying about such things. Your Father knows what you need. But put God's work first, and these things will be yours as well.

My little group of disciples, don't be afraid! Your Father wants to give you the kingdom. Sell what you have and give the money to the poor. Make yourselves moneybags that never wear out. Make sure your treasure is safe in heaven, where thieves cannot steal it and moths cannot destroy it. Your heart will always be where your treasure is.

Visual aids

Buy some Fairtrade products from your local supermarket. Make a note of the prices compared to similar products.

Explain that Thomas Clarkson took these words very seriously. He gave up the chance of a comfortable career in the church to spend his life campaigning against slavery. His 'treasure' lay in winning freedom for enslaved Africans, and his famous 'African chest' pointed to different ways of buying and selling. Christians like him (and others) started this early Fairtrade movement, 200 years ago, to give free Africans the chance to make a living for themselves.

Show Abolitionist images from the time, doing an internet search for 'Abolitionist sugar campaign'.

Explain that Fairtrade products are sold today in our local shops, but they sometimes cost more because more of the money is paid to the people who produced them.

What questions do your pupils think Christians today would ask themselves if they found bananas on sale in a supermarket at 99p for ordinary ones and £1.50 for Fairtrade? What do they think Christians might do, and why? What do they think about this?

Numeracy

Does your school run a Fairtrade tuck shop? Fairtrade Fortnight is a useful opportunity for schools to focus on the ethics of fair trade. Traidcraft's *World of Difference* is an excellent series of lessons for primary schools about fair trade today, with problem-solving maths activities involving sugar, raisins, rice and honey. See www.traidcraftschools.co.uk/making-a-world-of-difference-introductory-powerpoints.

Circle Time

Note

Be careful to avoid material that today would be considered offensive or hurtful to those of African heritage.

Age 5–11: Making a fairer world

This session is about why fair trade is so important. It could be used as an introduction to running a school Fairtrade week.

Preparation

Prepare a 'bad science' experiment (see below). You will also need two lists of maths questions, some Fairtrade products and a globe.

Introduction

Run a patently unfair science experiment. Say, 'We're going to study how air resistance affects how things fall to the ground.' Take two pieces of paper of different colours, screw one up in a ball and drop them both to see which hits the ground first (the one screwed up in a ball). Then discuss whether (for example) 'blue paper falls more quickly'. In discussion, establish that this was bad science because we should only change one factor—either air resistance or colour—before comparing like with like. Real scientists have to be very strict about keeping their tests fair.

Call up two volunteers (children who have a good sense of humour) for a quiz to see 'who's best at Numeracy'. Ask each one different questions, with one child's set being obviously much harder than the other's. Discuss the unfairness of the quiz and apologise to the 'loser'.

Development

Explain that 'fairness' is a strange concept. It's almost as if we're born with the idea that things ought to be fair. If you put two small children together and give one a sweet, the other one will expect to be given one, too—because it's 'fair'.

Ask pupils (in pairs) to discuss what being 'fair' means and feed back to the class. Expect answers to be along the lines of 'everyone being treated the same'—but is life fair in that sense? Why should we all be treated the same? People live longer if they live in Britain rather than many poorer countries. (Show the globe.) Some children never go to school. They have to work from a young age and don't live as long as we do. Some countries have lots of wars. Is that fair for the people who live there? It's not, but that's the way our world is. So why might we still want things to be fair?

Discuss in pairs again and feed back to the class. (Expect answers along the lines of 'because everyone's important'.)

How could *we* make things fairer for children in poorer countries who don't get the chance to go to school? Does the class have any ideas? (Expect the answer 'Give them money'.) Sometimes, the best way to help someone who's got no money isn't to give them money. Instead, we could help them to make their own money. We could help to pay for the teachers or the school so that children can learn, get cleverer and make a living when they're older. That's why we encourage fair trade. When we buy Fairtrade chocolate or bananas or other products at the shops, more of our money goes to help the people who grew them, so that they can afford to have a school in their village, or a clinic, or clean water.

∞ Prayer ∞

Father God, we don't live in a fair world, but everybody's important to you. Thank you for the things we have here, but don't let us forget the others. We all share the same planet and we all need each other. Amen

• Thought for today •

'Count your blessings, name them one by one.'

Unit 10

Charitable giving

Background for teachers

Children will be familiar with annual celebrity-driven campaigns that raise money for good causes. Charities welcome all donations but the contributions that make a real difference come from the people who make a regular commitment to giving over the long term. This helps the charity to plan ahead, knowing that its income will cover the long-term costs. If the regular donation is Gift Aided, that increases the value of the gift even more because the charity can claim back the tax. This is an old idea: just as most Muslims will be familiar with the regular obligation to offer alms (*Zakat*), many Christians will know of the 'tithe', a regular donation of ten per cent from personal income. (The collection of agricultural offerings for the church in 'tithe barns' was a feature of British country life right into the early 20th century.)

Should we encourage school pupils to give regularly to charity? It may not be easy or practical for some (due to family circumstances or beliefs), but schools can still demonstrate the value of commitment by establishing long-term links with a chosen charity, engaging with its values and supporting its work over a sustained period. Harvest festival is an excellent time for schools to explore connections between thankfulness and generosity in collective worship.

There is also the option of making a 'global link' with schools in other parts of the world. Partnerships of this sort always need to be handled with diplomacy and sensitivity, to avoid perpetuating the unspoken assumption that we in the West are 'rich' and the others are 'poor' simply because we have more money. The economic differences in income and expenditure may conceal other realities: children in 'undeveloped' parts of the world often have a much richer idea of responsibility in their families and communities than we do.

Story: Visiting time

The hospital ward was busy. Some patients were lying in their beds, surrounded by visitors, while others sat with their books or magazines, hoping that somebody would be visiting them soon. Half-whispered conversations buzzed around bedsides as presents were given and news passed on.

Mr Anderson didn't have any guests this afternoon, but he didn't mind. Perhaps he could get some sleep. His old body felt so tired these days. He snuggled down beneath the covers and began to doze. Then, from nearby, came a voice.

'Excuse me. Are you Mr Anderson? Mr Philip Anderson?'

He opened his tired eyes to see a young woman in a white coat standing beside his bed, holding a clipboard. Who was she? He hadn't seen her before. 'Yes. That's me.'

She smiled. 'I'm Doctor Scott. I'm here to talk you through your operation. We've been able to bring it forward and we want to do it first thing tomorrow morning. Since we'd never met, I thought I'd come in to talk about what we're going to do. But I also recognised your name, and I wanted to say thank you.'

'Thank you? What for?'

'Because I think I know you from somewhere way back. About 30 years ago, you did something really important and it changed my life for the better.'

Mr Anderson frowned. 'Me? What did I do?'

'Well, back then, I lived in Zimbabwe and my family couldn't afford to send me to school. So my mother got in touch with a child sponsorship charity, and I think you're the person who ended up sponsoring me. You'd have known me as Catherine Mwemba… but I'm married now.'

Philip's mind raced down his hall of memories, trying to make sense. He remembered sponsoring several African children, but he couldn't even name the countries. Why was his mind so fuzzy? This was embarrassing.

'Catherine… Doctor…' he said, 'look, I'm sorry, I know I sponsored children, but it was a long time ago and it was my wife who did most of the organising. I know there were letters and photos going back and forth, and I did read them, so I know it happened… but, I'm sorry, I can't even remember your name. Are you sure we're the ones who did it?'

'Yes! I've checked your address and everything. For ten years, you sent £25 every month to the charity in my name. It made all the difference—and you kept giving it, for years. It was enough, and you helped me get to school. You paid for my teachers, my books and my computer. I went to college, passed my medical exams and got the qualifications I needed. So I was able to travel and got the job I needed. I came to work in Britain a few years ago. And you did it!' she enthused, patting him on the shoulder. She had a lovely smile.

Mr Anderson sighed. 'Well, I'm glad it all worked out for you. Sometimes, giving to charity feels like throwing money into a vast hole, and you never know if it makes a difference.' He stared at her. 'Now you're here. Remarkable!'

She smiled. 'Well, it certainly made a difference. Now I send money back home to my family in Zimbabwe every month.'

'But what are you doing here now?'

'Well, tomorrow, Mr Anderson, I'm going to be operating on your heart with my medical team. Do you know something about the heart? It quietly gets on with things and does its job. That's what

Reproduced with permission from *Valuing Money* by Chris Hudson (Barnabas in Schools, 2015) www.barnabasinschools.org.uk

your £25 a month did. It got on with helping me and my family to live—and that's why I'm here today, years later, ready to talk about your operation. Your regular giving to the charity gave my family a fresh start, and I'm going to do the same with your heart tomorrow. We're going to give it a fresh start.' She turned to the notes on her clipboard. 'Shall we talk about it?'

So they did.

Reproduced with permission from *Valuing Money* by Chris Hudson (Barnabas in Schools, 2015) www.barnabasinschools.org.uk

Religious Education

Age 5–7: The feeding of the 5000

A key Christian idea about giving is that the attitude of the individual giver is as important to God as the amount handed over. It's all to do with humility—recognising that every good gift originally comes from God, so 'charity' is simply giving some of it back. The story of the feeding of the 5000 (Matthew 14:13–21) gives an example of this, with the additional point that the most generous person in the story was a child, who saw his gift multiplied by a miracle.

Use the following script to retell the story through drama. Stand the children in a circle to play the In/Out Statues game. (They start by facing out of the circle. At an audible signal from you, they turn inwards to become statues feeling tired… hungry… worried… grumpy… lost… confused and so on. Younger children can play by sitting together and making faces.) Pick out some extravert pupils to play 'grumpy grown-ups' (disciples), who sit to one side. With the main group, tell the story, acting it together as you go. Say aloud the lines spoken by the different characters, with the pupils immediately repeating each line. To add a journey element, add responses such as 'Are we there yet?'

Bible link: Matthew 14:13–21 (paraphrased)

Paul was going to have a special day out. He packed his rucksack with a lunchbox and a bottle of drink and ran out of the house to follow his friends down the road. They'd all heard about this storyteller and they wanted to go and see him. The crowd were meeting by a big lake. Some of them went for a paddle, splashing each other with water. Then somebody said, 'The storyteller's this way!' So they started walking up a large hill. Where was the storyteller?

At the top of the hill, they were met by some grumpy grown-ups who faced them in a line, saying, 'What do you want?' The children replied, 'We're here to see the storyteller!' The grumpy grown-ups gave all sorts of excuses about why they couldn't stay, but the children insisted, 'That's not fair! We want to hear some stories!'

Then Jesus emerged from a tent, told off the grumpy grown-ups (who were his own disciples) for keeping the children away and spent a couple of hours telling his tales and chatting with people. After all the stories, it was starting to get a bit late. Some of the crowd were starting to get tired and hungry—especially the ones who'd had nothing at all to eat since breakfast. The disciples said, 'Jesus! You'd better stop and send them back now, before the shops shut. Some of these people need to buy some food.' Jesus said, 'You feed them!'

One disciple shouted to the crowd, 'Has anybody got any food to share?' All the grown-ups said nothing, but one child stood up. 'I'll share,' he said, and was brought forward to see Jesus, who picked up his lunchbox. There were five buttered bread rolls in there—very nice. And two bits of grilled fish—very nice. Thank you, Paul!

Jesus held up the bread rolls and fish and prayed, 'Blessed are you, Lord our God, who brings forth food from the ground! Oh, and thank you, Paul, too!' He put the packed lunch in a basket and started sharing it out to the crowd. People kept pulling out bread rolls and bits of fish. Paul's packed lunch seemed to be going an awfully long way—those bread rolls seemed to just keep on going. The baskets weren't getting empty. People kept eating and eating until they were full.

'Don't throw any away,' said Jesus. 'We mustn't waste food.' So the disciples picked up all the spare rolls and bits of fish. In all, the leftover rolls and fish filled twelve baskets! 'What's going on?' asked the disciples. 'What's going on?' asked the crowd.

'Ah,' said Jesus, 'it's all to do with a secret. Love God and love your neighbour as you love yourself. Isn't it funny how, when we start sharing, there's food enough for everybody? When we share, God makes sure there's enough for all!'

Discuss

- Why do you think the adults didn't want to share their food? What sorts of things might they have said when the disciples came round asking if anyone was willing to share?
- What might have prompted the boy to offer his own packed lunch?
- Apart from food, what else might we share with people? (Our toys, our time, our friends…?)
- How might our world be different if nobody shared—or if everybody did?
- What do you think Jesus wanted everyone to remember about the day?
- Do you think this is a story that people need to hear about today? Why?

Extension

Ask pupils to draw the basket of loaves and fishes under the title 'Sharing'. To the left of their picture, in thought bubbles, they can add the reactions of the boy, one of the disciples and somebody in the crowd when the disciples ask for donations. To the right, they can add their own reactions to the end of the story.

Set the writing task of retelling the story, first from the boy's point of view and then from the point of view of one of the disciples. Are there any points where they would disagree?

Age 7–11: The widow's mite

In biblical times, charitable donations were channelled through the temple in Jerusalem, and every religious Jew was expected to pay the minimum temple tax of two 'minas' on an annual basis. This lesson dramatises an incident in the temple, related in Mark's Gospel.

Bible link: Mark 12:41–44

Jesus was sitting in the temple near the offering box and watching people put in their gifts. He noticed that many rich people were giving a lot of money. Finally, a poor widow came up and put in two coins that were worth only a few pennies. Jesus told his disciples to gather around him. Then he said:

I tell you that this poor widow has put in more than all the others. Everyone else gave what they didn't need. But she is very poor and gave everything she had. Now she doesn't have a penny to live on.

Begin with a 'cross the circle' game about gifts. Ask the pupils to stand in a circle, then to cross it 'if you've ever had a brilliant gift', 'if you've ever had a really rubbish gift' and 'if you've ever been given a gift that wasn't appreciated'. Invite them to share a few stories. Ask the pupils to sit down, and then lead off, using mime to pass 'gifts' around the circle. They can show by the way they handle each 'gift' how big, small, heavy or precious it is.

Explain the background to the story—the Jerusalem temple of two millennia ago. Display pictures or images from the internet to give a sense of the space. The temple's 'Court of the Women' was the place where everyone (including men) would come to bring their financial gifts for God, to be used for the work of the temple, which included caring for the poor. Offerings were placed in 13 bronze jars, or 'trumpets', in ascending order of importance from left to right—and the money that people put in would make quite a noise. It was sometimes called 'sounding the trumpets' (see Matthew 6:2). Jars 3–8 contained donations for burnt sacrifices. Temple staff were in attendance, with pilgrims lining up to make their donations.

1	2	3	4	5	6	7	8	9	10	11	12	13
Temple tax	Temple tax	Pigeons	Doves	Wood	Incense	Lambs	Calves	Gold	Extras	Extras	Extras	Extras

Sort the class into four named groups:

• Priests

• Temple guards

• Farmers/fishermen

• Businessmen

Play the 'fruit salad' game, where members of each group have to swap places when you call out their name . Everyone swaps places when you call the word 'Charity'.

Next, establish a different character for each group of people. Priests wear fine robes and enjoy feeling important. Temple guards are in charge of security: they're full of attitude, looking around suspiciously. Nobody messes with them. The other two groups are ordinary people, making their annual pilgrimage to the temple.

Talk together, answering the following questions to get 'in character'. What kind of journey did you make to Jerusalem? What kind of year has it been for you—prosperous or not? Everyone has to pay the basic temple tax in Jars 1 or 2, but some can pay more to show how successful they've been and how grateful they are. What have the different types of people got to show for themselves? What would they be doing or carrying? How would they walk? Would their gifts be burdensome? Ask everybody, 'in character', to walk in random directions, avoiding others, following pathways and carrying props if necessary.

Then create this scenario for improvised dramatisation.

• Place priests in a line from left to right, to receive gifts for the temple. Give each one a musical instrument to play, showing the importance of the gift being received.

• 'Givers' (farmers, fishermen and businessmen) come in two lines and must decide what kind of gift they are bringing and where it is going to go.

• Temple guards keep the 'givers' in line, letting them through but keeping an eye out for thieves and pickpockets.

Once each 'giver' has presented a gift, they should find a space, watch what's going on and applaud any particularly impressive gifts. Everyone must keep in role as the gifts are brought, until everyone has 'given'.

After the improvisation, settle everybody down, sitting together, then retell the story of Jesus and his disciples in the temple. First, imagine what they might have noticed and talked about; second, point out what Jesus noticed—how some people brought large gifts and others small. Then one little old lady, a poor widow with no one to look after her and protect her, offered a small gift, but it was obviously all she had to give. Jesus expressed his amazement, saying that she gave more than everyone else—because it was all she had.

Discuss

- What do you think is the key message of this story?
- What might it be saying about generosity? (You don't have to be rich to have a generous heart.)
- If Jesus had spoken with the old woman afterwards, what do you think he might have said to her? How might she have replied?

Ask the pupils to draw a pair of scales, with a small purse on one side weighing more than a big bag of money on the other. Set them the task of summing up the message of the story in no more than ten words.

Circle Time

Age 5–11: What does it mean to be 'caring'?

This session is about what it means to show practical care for others. It could also be used as an introduction to a child sponsorship scheme or other practical aid project.

Preparation

You will need a display board and pen.

Introduction

Draw a simple cartoon desert island on the board, with a palm tree and a stick man near the tree. Discuss as a group what it would be like to have to go and live there.

In pairs, pupils should discuss the most important things a person would need on a desert island. What would they miss having most of all? In feedback, draw out the idea that the one thing we would miss most of all would be having other people who care for us.

Development

Explain that people are 'social'. Most of the time, we naturally like to be with other people who care for us. In pairs, pupils should discuss how we know that someone cares for us. Feed back and list answers on the board, drawing out the idea that 'caring' is something you do, not just feel.

Set the challenge of creating freeze-frame statues, in pairs, to show someone caring for somebody else. Ask pairs to display their statues, and ask questions about the different types of care being shown in each situation.

In the Bible, a man called Paul wrote about what it means to be really caring, and he called it 'love'.

Bible link: 1 Corinthians 13:4–8 (paraphrased)

Love is patient, and it is kind. It isn't jealous or envious. It doesn't boast, and it isn't proud. Love isn't selfish and it isn't rude. Love doesn't want to always have its own way. Love isn't irritable and it isn't grumpy. Love doesn't keep dragging up the bad things people do and waving them in their faces. Love can't stand it when people are unfair, and love is always glad when the truth comes out at last. Love is always loyal, no matter what, always believes the best of people, and always stands up for them. Love goes on for ever.

Jesus told his followers to care for other people as they cared for themselves. A school can only be a truly happy school if everybody cares for each other like that. We all need to try to show more care for each other every day.

Talk about how we can show practical care for someone living in another country who needs help. This could lead into a discussion of child sponsorship or a similar project. If so, try to move the discussion beyond ideas about simply giving money. What about writing letters and taking an interest in the sponsored child's life?

∞ Prayer ∞

Father God, help me to learn how to care for other people in the ways that Paul wrote about. Amen

• Thought for today •

'Love is patient, and it is kind.'

Assemblies

Assembly 1

Don't be fooled!

For years, manufacturers have played on the 'collecting' instinct of children: customers buy packs of products unseen (for example, coins, models, stickers or trading cards) in the hope of collecting the set. In terms of probability, it is incredibly hard to collect the complete set without heavily trading in swaps, because the more of the set they collect, the more likely it is that the next pack they buy will include some that they've already got. If your school is plagued by the latest collecting craze, use this assembly to open children's eyes to how the scam works.

Preparation

You will need a display board and marker pen; plastic pound coin money; a pack of playing cards and a few examples of trading cards or whatever is being collected by pupils at the moment.

Introduction

Show a trading card, asking pupils to put up their hands if they are collecting the set. Ask how much they cost in local shops. Show a pack of playing cards. Explain that this assembly isn't about a card trick; it's about explaining a trick that gets played on children—and it might even save them some money.

Development

Ask some volunteers to shuffle the cards. Then say that you are collecting just the full set of hearts and you're going to 'buy' sets of ten cards for £1.00 every time. How many sets of ten will you need to buy to get all the hearts, as there are 52 cards in a pack, including 13 hearts? Ask for suggested answers from the audience, noting them down on the display board.

Using the plastic pound coins, buy ten cards, show them, and mark on the display board which hearts appear. (The cards you've bought must go back in the pack for reshuffling, to maintain the random element.) Buy another set of ten, again noting any hearts. Repeat at least five times, noting any 'doubles' when the same hearts cards keeps appearing.

You won't be able to get all the hearts in assembly time, because it will take quite a lot of tries to do so. Each attempt carries a probability of 13/52 (or 1/4) of getting a heart, no matter how many times the exercise is repeated, but the chance of getting one particular card, such as the 3 of hearts, stays at 1/52. It could take you 52 attempts, and even then it might not be enough. It doesn't get easier as you approach the full set: in fact, it gets harder. Challenge children to try it at home and then come back to tell you how long it actually takes.

Explain that all the 'collecting' crazes work on the same principle and it's a great way to make money out of children. We all tend to think the collecting will get easier when we've got nearly all the cards—but it doesn't. Ask a few volunteers to say how many packs of trading cards they have bought. How many are there in the full set? Have they got the set yet? (No!)

Say that Jesus told his followers to watch out for 'wolves in sheep's clothing', people who promise one thing when actually they're after something different. Jesus said that he was something of a collector himself, going out of his way to find all the people whose lives were going wrong, like a shepherd looking for lost sheep. But he was a good shepherd, a collector of people who became his friends, not a collector of things.

The apostle Paul later said that the only things worth collecting are not actually things: they are faith, hope and love.

Explain that collecting things can be great fun, but, before we part with our pocket money, we should ask ourselves, 'Do I really need this thing, just so that it can be part of a set? Is it worth having a full set? Why not just have the ones I like? Or why not collect things when I know exactly what I'm getting before I part with my money?'

Here's a weirder thought: why not try collecting friends instead, by sharing toys and games instead of everyone having to buy their own?

∞ Prayer ∞

Lord Jesus, thank you for being the greatest collector of all. Collecting is fun but, when it gets silly, remind me to only collect the most important things. Amen

• Thought for today •

Having more stuff doesn't make us feel better. Only people and God can do that.

Assembly 2

It's all in the detail

It's easy to say 'Yes' to an offer before realising that there may be hidden consequences. Financial agreements involve a lot of 'small print', easily ignored but sometimes highly significant later on. This classic cautionary tale about the invention of chess provides due warning about checking the details when we make a promise—especially if those details involve numbers.

Preparation

You will need a chessboard and chess pieces; some grains of dry rice; a pocket calculator or computer calculator display.

Introduction

Say: Have you ever played chess? It's a great game, like a small battle with soldiers. All the pieces have their special moves. There's no luck involved: it's all skill. The really great players plan several moves in advance. That's a good lesson for life—think ahead!

There's a strange story about the man who invented it and the man to whom he sold it. It's a story about a game, but it's also a story about thinking ahead and not saying 'Yes' to the first thing you hear.

Development

Tell the following story.

There was once a great king in India who was feeling bored and wanted a mental challenge, so he asked a local mathematician to invent a new game for him. 'Make it something exciting!' said the king. 'Something to get the old mind working again!'

The mathematician went away for a few weeks, then returned with a large board of 64 black and white squares and a box. 'What's in there?' asked the king, mystified. The mathematician opened the box and placed 32 black and white playing pieces on the board. 'These are two armies, your Excellency,' declared the mathematician. 'There is the infantry (the foot soldiers), the cavalry (the horse soldiers), the elephants and the chariots. Each type of piece has its own special set of moves. Playing this game can be learned in a few hours, but playing it well may take you a lifetime.'

The king tried it out and was very pleased. 'What can I pay you?' he asked.

The mathematician looked around the room mysteriously to check they were alone, then said, 'I have a little proposition for you, Excellency. I would like to be paid in grains of rice.' He had a few grains with him and led the king over to the chess board. 'See, your Excellency?' He placed one grain of rice in the first square, then two in the second, then four in the next one. 'It's just simple doubling, your Excellency. All I'd like for payment is the amount of rice created if you keep doubling the number each time, for all the squares on the board.'

'Is that all?' said the king. 'A few grains of rice? No gold? No jewels? It's a deal!' He brought a servant in, wrote and signed a letter of agreement, and the promise was made. The mathematician looked rather pleased as he shuffled out with the letter.

Then the servant said, 'Your Excellency is a most generous man.'

'Why?'

'To give away so much rice.'

'Really?'

'Your Excellency, would you allow me to show you exactly how much?' The servant started making some calculations on a piece of paper. All he did was start with 1. Then he doubled it. Then he did it again and again. 1, 2, 4, 8, 16, 32, 64... the total was getting rather large. He had to use more pieces of paper. (Can any of you do it in your head? See how far you can go.)

After an hour, the servant handed a very large stack of paper to the king. 'That, your Excellency, is the number of grains of rice you promised him. It's about 18 trillion grains. Your Excellency, we don't have that much rice in our kingdom. If we piled it all up, that amount of rice would be larger and taller than the highest mountain in India!'

'What?' asked the king. 'I didn't know!'

'Your Excellency, if I may be so bold... next time anyone asks you to sign anything, check the details—or ask me to do it.'

'I will!' said the king. 'But wait until I've found that mathematician. When I do... it'll be off with his head!'

It's a silly story and probably not true, but there's a special message in there: be careful with your promises, and be careful when people ask you to sign your name to things. As we get older and have the chance to spend more money, we'll sometimes be asked to sign agreements or give our security details to people over the internet—and we should always be careful. Just because something looks good, it doesn't mean it is, whether we see it in a shop or on a computer screen. Be careful before clicking the box marked 'YES'. Have someone you trust checking it out, too. This is why we do Maths in school—to prepare us for life, so that we can work out these sorts of things for ourselves.

Jesus told his followers to be 'as wise as snakes and as innocent as doves' (Matthew 10:16). Snakes were thought to be clever—so you be clever, too, and don't get tricked like that silly king!

∞ Prayer ∞

Lord Jesus, thank you that our minds are learning all sorts of things all the time. Help me to make the most of my time in school so that I can make the right choices when I'm older. Amen

• Thought for today •

A question: what can Numeracy teach us, that's not about numbers?

Assembly 3
Doing the right thing

Bible link: Matthew 21:1–17

The story of Holy Week begins with the procession on Palm Sunday, as Jesus and his disciples entered Jerusalem, a crowded city full of political plots and dense intrigues that must have felt worlds away from life near Lake Galilee. On Palm Sunday, people were wondering about Jesus. Was he planning to drive out the Romans, or what? Instead, Jesus staged an unorthodox demonstration, attacking the street market set up by the temple authorities in an area traditionally reserved for Gentiles to pray to the Jewish God. (Gentiles weren't allowed any nearer to the temple precincts, on pain of death.) The market seems a strange target, but it was evidently of great value to the authorities, so Jesus was hitting them where it hurt.

This assembly takes a child's-eye view of the main moments. (For an alternative retelling with percussion instruments and a lot more noise, use this script from the Barnabas in Schools website: www.barnabasinschools.org.uk/percussion-palm-sunday.)

Preparation

You will need pictures of Palm Sunday and some oranges in a fruit basket. If you know British Sign Language, use it to teach a few words to the audience in your introduction.

Introduction

Once everyone is seated, let them sit quietly for a few seconds. Then say, 'Quiet here, isn't it? It's nice to have a bit of peace and quiet sometimes. But for some people, it's always too quiet. If you can't hear very well, then you miss out on a whole world of sounds. This is a story about a very noisy day that isn't noisy for one boy—until the very end.'

Development

Use the following script.

Hello. My name's Reuben. Excuse me if the words come out wrong, but you'll soon find out why. It all started at Sunday lunch time. I was outside the big city of Jerusalem, selling oranges for my dad. It's what my family does: we sell oranges. We've got a farm a few miles away from the city, and oranges are what we grow best. Dad says we're good at it, but that's the problem, see—because I can't hear him when he says anything. Not a word.

I'm deaf, you see. My ears don't work. I wasn't born like it, but I was three when I had this sickness and now... I'm here, but I can't hear. Get it? So my eyes have to work hard to take everything in. I read lips. I look at what people seem to be saying and guess what they mean. I'm normally right. When we're selling oranges, I just use my fingers to show how many coins I want for an orange. It usually works—and my Maths is brilliant!

On Sunday, there were big crowds and I saw a whole load of people coming into the city through the Roman Gate, waving giant leaves and all sorts. Some of them were making a big fuss about someone riding a donkey—but who was he? No idea. They all marched their way into the city, following the man on the donkey. Then Dad touched me on the shoulder, pointed to the basket and did the thumbs-up, which means, 'Off you go, lad. Follow that lot and sell some more oranges.' So I did.

Our city's got lots of thin winding streets, some of them dark tunnels. There are places where it's not safe to go, but I know the safe places and soon I was up with the crowd again, going from person to person as we walked, holding up the basket and the fingers, smiling and selling a few. I'm good at selling!

Then the crowd went up some big steps and we were out in the sun again, in the big open courtyard by the temple. That's the place where no one used to be allowed to sell anything, where foreigners used to pray to our God—Romans, Greeks, Ethiopians, Egyptians—but that changed a few years ago, and anyone can sell there if you pay for your pitch. My dad doesn't. I don't know why. So the courtyard's a big market now. There's traders selling sheep, goats, pigeons, doves, water, souvenirs, bread rolls, anything! There are the money changers, too. They take the Roman money and swap it for temple money if you pay them. They say only temple money is good enough for God.

So I turn up in the courtyard with my basket… and suddenly it's all going mad! I slip on some smashed eggs. There's animals charging around, birds up in the air, flapping their feathers, people panicking, people pushing and shoving—and I can't see a thing because they're all in my way! Then suddenly, I get hit in the face by some flying bread rolls. I duck down and grab one, then… whoosh… I see a shower of something sparkly and there's silver coins rolling everywhere. Someone treads on my foot and, whoops, there goes my basket! What's happening?

Then it all calms down a bit and I check I've still got my money bag. I can see somebody arguing with someone else. It's the man who was riding the donkey outside. There's no donkey now, but he's standing there saying something to a temple guard, who turns and stomps away. There are lots of children running up to him, some of them younger than me. The man is smiling because they're jumping around, dancing around him in a circle and saying something—but I don't know what it is.

So I take a few steps closer to see better. Then the man sees me and, with his fingers, he's saying, 'It's all right. Come over here.' So I do. There's grown-ups watching, so I know it's all right. He stands me right in front of everybody while he's talking, though I don't know why. Then he looks down and, with his big hands, he touches me on both sides of the head…

IT HURTS! The world shakes and I feel giddy, but he grabs me by the shoulders so I don't fall over. I can hear his talking and it HURTS! Everything in my ears HURTS! I can hear people shouting, singing, arguing, and all of it is bouncing around INSIDE MY HEAD, and I try to cover my ears to make it stop. Then he stands in front of me, crouches down so that I can see his face and see his lips moving. And quietly, he whispers something…

After that, I found my basket and went back to see Dad. All the oranges had gone, but so what? He started telling me off for losing them, but it was wonderful! It was brilliant! Do you know why? BECAUSE I CAN HEAR MY DAD'S VOICE!

∞ Prayer ∞

Lord Jesus, on Palm Sunday you put people first, before everything else, including money. It might have made you some enemies, but the children loved you and sang their praises to God. Thank you for helping others and for being so brave. Show us how to be brave, too. Help us to do the right thing, just like you did. Amen

• Thought for today •

Doing the right thing might get you into trouble—but it's still the right thing.

Appendices

Appendix 1

'Ethical' number challenges and investigations with money

Numeracy doesn't have to be morally neutral. The 'What-if Learning' project (www.whatiflearning. co.uk) suggests that a Christian understanding of life can make a positive difference to teaching and learning. Teachers of all faiths and beliefs have found this approach helpful when considering how their subjects might contribute to a child's Spiritual, Moral, Social and Cultural education. So how could Numeracy investigations about money show the values of faith, hope and love? Here are some possibilities that you might want to adapt to suit the needs of your own pupils. All provide opportunities for challenging Numeracy investigations, working with money, and adding an ethical dilemma for discussion during the plenary part of the lesson.

For a download of these problems and others, with suggestions for simplification and extensions, go to www.barnabasinschools.org.uk/9780857461216.

Here's a useful tip for teachers: before setting a problem-solving task for your pupils, try doing it yourself for five minutes without looking at the answers (on pages 112–116). It's fascinating to notice which key bits of knowledge or skills are dredged up from our own memories when we tackle problems like this, and it can illuminate any difficulties (or useful steps) for our pupils as well.

Faith

Faith makes us sure of what we hope for and gives us proof of what we cannot see.

HEBREWS 11:1

'If you had faith no larger than a mustard seed, you could tell this mountain to move from here to there. And it would. Everything would be possible for you.'

MATTHEW 17:20–21

'Faith' is a hypothesis, an experiment of trust that uses a smaller bit of information to draw conclusions about something greater, and tests it. All mathematical investigations that involve 'trial-and-improve' methods exercise faith by using strategies that have worked for us before and might work again or might need to be improved. Before we make a purchase, faith asks questions such as:

- Do I trust what's been offered?
- Does it fit with what I already know?
- Will it be worth the money?
- Will I check my change afterwards?

Reproduced with permission from *Valuing Money* by Chris Hudson (Barnabas in Schools, 2015) www.barnabasinschools.org.uk

Activities

Easy money?

Paul wants to buy a new laptop and needs £150.00. The website of a loans company offers an 'easy' loan of £150.00 to be paid back at £5.00 a day (including interest) over 36 days.

- How much extra will the laptop cost if Paul takes out the loan?
- Do we think this is worth it?
- What could go wrong if Paul doesn't keep up with the daily payments?

Weekly instalments

Alvin is interested in finding out more about the human body. A weekly magazine is being advertised on TV. Over 52 weeks, the magazines combine to make a medical encyclopedia, and each magazine comes with a plastic 'body part' for building up a model of the human body. The first magazine costs £2.99, and after that they cost £5.99 each. Two large binders, to hold the magazines together, will cost another £9.99 each.

- Calculate the final cost of the complete encyclopedia and model.
- Do you think it's worth it?
- Do you think Alvin could buy the completed items cheaper elsewhere?

Fancy a banquet?

Show a menu from a local restaurant or takeaway that offers discounts for customers who buy the set meals instead of individual items.

Choose one set meal and work out the savings if customers buy it instead of buying the individual items.

- Is it worth it?
- Do you actually end up spending more, because it encourages you to have more items? Does that matter?

Develop this investigation further by planning the best possible value meal for four people, costing £40.00 in total.

Glug! Glug! Glug!

Most children need to drink about a litre of water a day in some way, and bottled water costs about £1.50 a litre.

- If Barak only drank bottled water, how much would that cost him per week?
- How much would it cost for a month (four weeks)?
- How much would it cost for a year (52 weeks)?
- How much would it cost for five years?
- Barak could drink water from the tap much more cheaply. Why do some people prefer buying bottled water?
- Do you think bottled water is worth all the extra packaging and cost? Why or why not?

Reproduced with permission from *Valuing Money* by Chris Hudson (Barnabas in Schools, 2015) www.barnabasinschools.org.uk

Checking your change

It's always important to check your change when shopping, so do you know how to count up quickly, like old-fashioned shop assistants? Suppose you give one pound for an item costing 65p. The shop assistant might pay the change by counting up from 65p—first giving you 5p ('That's 70p...'), then 10p ('80...'), 10p ('90...') and another 10p ('One pound!'). You should now be holding 35p.

In ten seconds or less (working with a partner and some plastic coins), work out the right change using this method if you handed over a £1.00 coin to buy:

- a comic at 75p
- a magazine at 85p
- a bag of sweets at 55p

Try a few more, then develop the challenge with a partner, setting them three different prices to see how fast they can work out the change for a £2.00 coin. Which mental Maths techniques work best?

Hope

> This hope is what saves us. But if we already have what we hope for, there is no need to keep on hoping. However, we hope for something we have not yet seen, and we patiently wait for it.
>
> ROMANS 8:24–25

> We gladly suffer, because we know that suffering helps us to endure. And endurance builds character, which gives us a hope.
>
> ROMANS 5:3–4

Hope is about having a goal, a clear sense of destination based on current knowledge. We can use Mathematics to explore or create a series of number patterns extrapolating from smaller to larger examples. When the pattern is expressed in formulae, we call it algebra.

When we start calculating percentages of money, this requires 'rounding' up or down. Pupils will need to be taught the basics of rounding, according to your school's scheme of work, before being set these tasks. If your school uses calculators, these can be very useful, but the ability to round numbers to the nearest two decimal places will still be necessary.

Activities

Saving together

A class decides together to save money for a local charity. Different pupils commit themselves to the following giving plans.

- Group A (six children) will each give 50p a week.
- Group B (seven children) will each give 75p a week.
- Group C (ten children) will each give £1.00 a week.

Reproduced with permission from *Valuing Money* by Chris Hudson (Barnabas in Schools, 2015) www.barnabasinschools.org.uk

- Group D (eight children) will each give £1.50 a week.
- The class teacher commits to giving £2.50 a week.

Calculate how much this class will have raised for the charity in one, two, four, eight and 16 weeks. (Before starting, ask pupils to discuss and jot down their estimates of how much this sort of 'giving plan' would raise in 16 weeks.)

- How can you use this information to calculate how much they could raise in 30 weeks?
- Can this information be presented in helpful graphs or tables?
- Do you know anyone who gives regularly to a charity? Why do you think they do this?

Getting interesting

A building society offers young savers the chance to make money. For every amount in the account, the building society will add 5 per cent interest at the end of each month. Yolanda deposits £12.00 at the beginning of January.

- What will this amount become at the end of January, after interest, and then in February?
- Following the same pattern, what will Yolanda have by the end of June, ready for the summer holiday, if she doesn't deposit any more money?
- Does anyone in the class save money anywhere?
- Do they know the interest rates?

Saving up or borrowing?

Akwesi's mum wants to take them both on holiday. It will cost £1404.00 'all in'. They can either save up the money week by week beforehand through the year or take a loan and pay it back afterwards.

- If they have six months before the holiday, how much will they need to save every month to cover the cost?
- If they borrow the money, it will mean paying back the loans company the £1404.00 over twelve months, but also adding five per cent interest on the whole amount. How much will the holiday eventually cost them if they do this?
- What questions do you think they'll be asking themselves as they weigh up the decision?

As an extension task for the more able, explore what might happen if Akwesi and his mum saved each month's holiday money in a special bank account that paid 5 per cent interest per month on the amount in the account. How much interest would they have after one month, two months and so on, up to six months? What would be the full amount in the account at the end of each month?

Love

> Love is patient, love is kind. It does not envy, it does not boast, it is not proud. It does not dishonour others, it is not self-seeking, it is not easily angered, it keeps no record of wrongs. Love does not delight in evil but rejoices with the truth. It always protects, always trusts, always hopes, always perseveres.
>
> 1 CORINTHIANS 13:4–7 (NIV)

Reproduced with permission from *Valuing Money* by Chris Hudson (Barnabas in Schools, 2015) www.barnabasinschools.org.uk

Activities

Flowers for Mum

Sanjeev earns £3.50 every week doing a paper round.

- If Sanjeev doesn't spend any of it, how long will it be before he has enough to buy his mother a large bouquet of flowers costing £24.99?
- Her birthday is in eight weeks' time. Does he have enough time? How do you know?
- When was the last time you gave something to your parents or carers?
- What sorts of gifts do you think they appreciate receiving from you most of all? Why?

Remembrance poppies

Before Remembrance Day, some pupils went from class to class, selling poppies for 20p each. They sold 120.

- How much did they raise for the Poppy Appeal?
- Georgiou's father used to be in the army, so he put in 50p but only took one poppy. 'Why didn't you buy two?' asked one of his classmates. How might he answer?
- Do you think they should have set a price of 20p a poppy? Without it, might some children have given more? What happens in your own school when people come to the classroom selling poppies?

Cake sale

Aleasha's class organised a cake sale. They sold 100 cakes and raised £32.75 for charity.

- How much money did each cake sell for, on average?
- The cakes had been bought in packs from a supermarket at £2.00 for ten. Calculate how much the class spent and how much they received back. Do you think the cake sale was worth the effort? Why?

A toilet for your birthday

Kamaljeet has decided that she has quite enough toys and clothes, so for her birthday this year she's telling all her friends and family to buy her a toilet for £42.00. Using a national charity, she wants them to help her buy a clean toilet for a school in a country where keeping clean and healthy isn't easy.

- Break up Kamaljeet's gift into different amounts of money. How many people would need to give £2.00 to make it happen? £3.00? £4.00? £5.00?
- She has said that she will also wash cars at £5.00 a time to buy another toilet. How many dirty cars will she need to wash?
- Washing a car takes about 30 minutes. How long will the task take in hours and minutes?
- What do you think about someone asking for this kind of birthday present?

Greeting card challenge

Among her family and friends, Keira wants to remember everyone's birthday but she's not sure how to do it best. An internet company sells a range of virtual greeting cards that can be

Reproduced with permission from *Valuing Money* by Chris Hudson (Barnabas in Schools, 2015) www.barnabasinschools.org.uk

customised and sent online. A year's subscription of £25.00 will allow Keira to send as many as she likes by email.

A pack of 15 greeting cards and envelopes costs £10.00. A single card costs £2.50, and a giant greeting card costs £9.50. In a year, she thinks she can afford around £40.00 on sending greetings to other people.

Begin this investigation by creating a family-and-friend network for Keira involving 20 people (two parents, three brothers, one grandparent, three aunts and eleven friends), perhaps showing it as a diagram. Then work out two different ways for Keira to spend her £40.00 celebrating birthdays, justifying your choices with a sentence or two.

Present swap

Tom and Sarah are friends at school who swapped Christmas presents they didn't want, but without telling their parents. Tom swapped his skateboard (costing £24.99) for Sarah's computer game (costing £39.99). Both children were happy, but their parents weren't and told them to give the presents back to each other.

- What was the difference in financial value between the two presents?
- Do you think the children or the parents were right, and why?
- Were the two items given by people who loved the two children? If so, should a gift be disposed of 'just like that' or should its recipient show more respect to the giver by keeping it?
- Would it be different if the two children were swapping toys that they'd bought with money they'd earned? Why?

Souvenir trading

Matthew visited Japan with his parents and was given some spending money. In a toyshop, he bought a pack of 30 exclusive trading cards for 1800 yen, which he immediately used for swaps when he was back in England. His mum was furious, saying that the Japanese cards were special souvenirs of a family holiday and shouldn't be swapped.

- Calculate the difference in financial value (150 yen = £1.00) between the cards sold in Britain (a pack of 15 for £2.50) and the ones sold in Japan.
- Was Matthew's mum right to be concerned? Why?
- Does keeping holiday souvenirs matter, if they help you collect the set of things you want when you're back home?
- Will the holiday memories disappear?
- Next time Matthew goes on holiday, how do you think the conversation with his parents might go if he is given spending money?

Tea party

Kylie, Shane, Cameron and Lucy are hosting a tea party for six elderly neighbours. Make a shopping list of what's needed and research the prices.

- What will they need to buy? What sorts of things will the guests want to eat and drink?
- What will the total cost be?
- How much will each child need to contribute?
- Can they save money by making some things themselves?
- For which tasks might they need adult help?

Reproduced with permission from *Valuing Money* by Chris Hudson (Barnabas in Schools, 2015) www.barnabasinschools.org.uk

Answers

Easy money?

Cost with loan is 36 x £5.00 = £180.00. Paul is paying £30.00 extra, an interest rate of 20 per cent.

Note: That's a bit steep, and, if he doesn't keep up with the payments, it'll be a lot more, because the interest on the unpaid amount might be much higher. Alternatively, if Paul saves the money first, putting aside £5.00 per day for 36 days, he'll be £30.00 better off when he eventually buys the laptop. (Which would we prefer to do, and why?)

Weekly instalments

Final cost is £2.99 + (£5.99 x 51) + (£9.99 x 2) =

£2.99 + £305.49 + £19.98 = **£328.46**

Note: How many people work out the total cost of this kind of magazine offer before signing up for it? 'Encyclopedias' like this can be bought very cheaply in discount bookshops, often with medical models attached. Nearly all these TV-advertised 'weekly instalment' purchase schemes are incredibly expensive. If someone likes building model kits, they should go to a model hobby shop.

Fancy a banquet?

Note: All answers depend on the local prices. Discuss why a restaurant or takeaway offers these deals. Are they able to offer these particular dishes more cheaply because the ingredients are cheaper and, if so, does that matter?

Glug! Glug! Glug!

Cost for a week is £1.50 x 7 = £10.50

Cost for a month is £10.50 x 4 = £42.00

Cost for a year is £10.50 x 52 = £546.00

Cost for five years is £546.00 x 5 = £2730.00

Note: That's an awful lot to pay for bottled water, which is usually taken straight from the local supply that provides tap water or, even worse, might be transported internationally. Concerns about the taste of local tap water (which may be 'hard' or 'soft') or added chemicals like fluoride (to harden teeth) may be genuine, but are they worth the extra expense of buying bottled?

Checking your change

For the comic: 25p

For the magazine: 15p

For the sweets: 45p

Note

Afterwards, it's worth discussing how confident we might be at challenging an adult shop assistant's maths if we think they've got it wrong. We are always advised to check our change before leaving a shop, so what's the best way to dispute the amount without starting an argument?

Reproduced with permission from *Valuing Money* by Chris Hudson (Barnabas in Schools, 2015) www.barnabasinschools.org.uk

Saving together

Using tables to lay out the information makes this kind of calculation easier. See how quickly your more able pupils realise that they're seeing a geometrical number sequence at work here, making calculations faster as we just double the previous answers. These progressive steps also allow us to calculate other totals quickly. For example, we can work out how much could be raised in seven weeks just by adding the totals for one, two and four weeks.

Tables like this have a long history in practical accountancy. Are they perhaps an early type of computer? Once you've worked this out as a class (perhaps with different groups being set the challenge of working out subtotals for groups A, B, C and D), discuss whether they would have expected to raise this much money over one long term.

Week	1	2	4	8	16
A **£0.50 x 6**	£3.00	£6.00	£12.00	£24.00	£48.00
B **£0.75 x 7**	£5.25	£10.50	£21.00	£42.00	£84.00
C **£1.00 x 10**	£10.00	£20.00	£40.00	£80.00	£160.00
D **£1.50 x 8**	£12.00	£24.00	£48.00	£96.00	£192.00
Teacher **£2.50**	£2.50	£5.00	£10.00	£20.00	£40.00
Total	**£32.75**	**£65.50**	**£131.00**	**£262.00**	**£524.00**

Reproduced with permission from *Valuing Money* by Chris Hudson (Barnabas in Schools, 2015) www.barnabasinschools.org.uk

Getting interesting

£12.00 + (5 per cent of £12.00 = £0.60) = £12.60 (end of January)

£12.60 + (5 per cent of £12.60 = £0.63) = £13.23 (end of February)

£13.23 + (5 per cent of £13.23 = £0.66) = £13.89 (end of March)

£13.89 + (5 per cent of £13.89 = £0.69) = £14.58 (end of April)

£14.58 + (5 per cent of £14.58 = £0.73) = £15.31 (end of May)

£15.31 + (5 per cent of £15.31 = £0.77) = £16.08 (end of June)

Saving up or borrowing?

Saving £1404.00 over six months will mean putting by £234.00 per month. Borrowing £1404.00 at 5 per cent interest = £70.20 extra. If they take the loan, the holiday will finally cost them £1404.00 + £70.20 = £1474.20.

Extension task: The running totals would look something like this, depending on approaches to rounding numbers to two decimal places. This demonstrates why saving instead of borrowing can make a real financial difference when planning a big expenditure. With saving, the interest rates work in your own favour, not that of the person lending you the money.

Saving like this, Akwesi and his mum could either put by less than £234.00 each month, and still have enough to cover the cost, or have some useful spending money thanks to all that added interest.

Note

More able pupils may benefit from being taught how to use a basic Excel spreadsheet to calculate continuous changes over a set period. Do your pupils like the idea of saving and getting interest, as opposed to paying extra for buying quickly by borrowing money?

End of month	1	2	3	4	5	6
Total in account	234.00	245.70	491.99	750.59	1022.12	1307.23
5% interest	11.70	12.29	24.60	37.53	51.11	65.36
New payment		234.00	234.00	234.00	234.00	234.00
New total	245.70	491.99	750.59	1022.12	1307.23	1606.59

Reproduced with permission from Valuing Money by Chris Hudson (Barnabas in Schools, 2015) www.barnabasinschools.org.uk

Flowers for Mum

Yes, Sanjeev does have enough time. He can do it like this.

Week 1	Week 2	Week 3	Week 4	Week 5	Week 6	Week 7	Week 8
£3.50	£7.00	£10.50	£14.00	£17.50	£21.00	£24.50	£28.00

Remembrance poppies

The class raised 120 x £0.20 = £24.00.

Discuss whether it's better to have a set price or a 'minimum donation'. Considering who the money is going to, or if we had some personal connection to the charity, do we think we would give more?

Cake sale

Selling price was £32.75 / 100 = approximately 33p per cake.

Money spent: £2.00 / 10 = a cost of 20p per cake.

That's a good profit of 13p per cake. However, making the cakes at home would probably be more fun and might generate even greater profits. Calculating exactly how many cakes can be made from one set of cake ingredients could be an intriguing homework task for some parents and children. Does your school have a cookery club?

Note: some supermarket chains might offer free cakes for charitable fundraising if asked nicely. A letter to a supermarket could be an interesting class literacy task using persuasive writing.

A toilet for your birthday

21 people need to give £2.00 each (14 people need to give £3.00, eleven people £4.00 and nine people £5.00). Kamaljeet will need to wash nine cars, which will take her four hours and 30 minutes.

Note: This activity lends itself to an open-ended exploration of 'How many ways can we make £42.00?' Expect your more able pupils to invent increasingly strange methods.

Present swap

The financial difference between the two presents is £15.00, but the difference in emotional value might be greater.

Reproduced with permission from *Valuing Money* by Chris Hudson (Barnabas in Schools, 2015) www.barnabasinschools.org.uk

Souvenir trading

The 1800 yen = £12.00 for 30 Japanese trading cards, while 30 English cards cost £5.00. That's a difference of £7.00, proving that the Japanese cards are more expensive. Afterwards, Matthew might have done some clever swaps (for example, three English cards for one Japanese) but he wouldn't get those Japanese cards back.

Tea party

Note: Researching prices makes for some active, practical homework in the previous week, and you can collate responses for use in the following week's lesson. Expect pupils to be surprised by the range of prices for the same product in different shops.

Reproduced with permission from *Valuing Money* by Chris Hudson (Barnabas in Schools, 2015) www.barnabasinschools.org.uk

Appendix 2

Going deeper with money in school

How can schools justify adding an ethical dimension to teaching about numeracy and money when there are so many other demands on the timetable? Numeracy lessons are necessarily focused on topics that explore and apply the mechanics of number-crunching. There may be momentary opportunities for discussing the human consequences of calculating solutions for real-life problems (such as planning the cost of a meal or a day out), but we won't find much time for ethical discussion about money unless we plan for it differently.

How? Probably the best solution is either to have a weekly problem-solving lesson that puts more focus on using and applying mathematical skills and understanding or, alternatively, to plan a series of cross-curricular lessons for a whole-school 'Money Week' (or fortnight) at a set time every year. (Planning a series of RE lessons on financial issues is easier: see pages 7–9.)

So what investigations could we organise for a school Money Week? A number of financial institutions and charities now provide excellent free teaching materials for schools. These materials can be very good at identifying and clarifying the choices we all face as individuals when handling money, but most avoid tackling awkward moral and spiritual questions. One glorious exception is Alvin Hall's book for children, *Show Me the Money!* (Dorling Kindersley, 2008). In one section ('The best things in life are free!') he writes:

Money helps people meet their basic needs for food, clothing, shelter, and health. More money can help people get more of the pleasures that make life less hard (like dishwashers) and more fun (like holidays). Beyond that, money doesn't tend to make people any happier. Sometimes we need more time, not more money. After all, you can't put a price on a hug from a friend or a glorious sunset.

This kind of philosophy doesn't normally enter the classroom during Maths lessons, so make the most of this cross-curricular topic, consider its broader possibilities regarding national initiatives such as Every Child Matters, and plan for some challenging fun.

For resources beyond this book, do visit the Barnabas in Schools website (www.barnabasinschools. org.uk). Also, make yourself familiar with the Personal Finance Education Group website (www. pfeg.org), which offers excellent free schemes of work that connect calculations to wider issues. Their Financial Education Planning Framework for ages 3–11 (subtitled 'Spend it, save it, give it, get it?') includes powerful 'I can…' pupil statements that progressively stretch further into thinking about money. For example, its targets for ages 7–9 include:

Role of charities		
I know what charities are for and what some might do.	I can explain how charities can help others.	I understand why I might, or might not, want to give money to a charity.

Downloadable resources such as 'Drip Drip Drip—a water themed financial education resource for primary teachers' provide creative class topics for busy teachers.

Index of Bible links

Summary of Bible passages

Illustrations

Unit 1: Zimbabwean million dollar note

Unit 2: Golden guinea from 1698

© Simon Smith 2015. Reproduced with permission from *Valuing Money* by Chris Hudson (Barnabas in Schools, 2015) www.barnabasinschools.org.uk

Unit 3: Chinese yuan from 400BC

Unit 4: Coin defaced by the Suffragette movement

Unit 5: Pretend money

© Simon Smith 2015. Reproduced with permission from *Valuing Money* by Chris Hudson (Barnabas in Schools, 2015) www.barnabasinschools.org.uk

Unit 6: Debit card

Unit 7: Tulip and bulb ('Semper Augustus')

© Simon Smith 2015. Reproduced with permission from *Valuing Money* by Chris Hudson (Barnabas in Schools, 2015) www.barnabasinschools.org.uk

Unit 8: One pound note from 1823

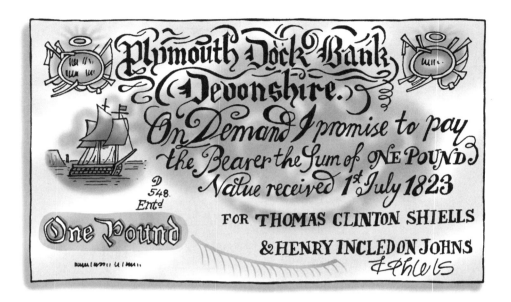

Unit 8: Five pound note from 1760

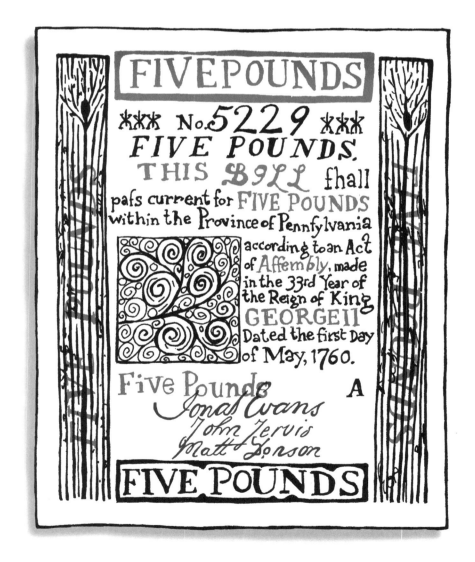

© Simon Smith 2015. Reproduced with permission from *Valuing Money* by Chris Hudson (Barnabas in Schools, 2015) www.barnabasinschools.org.uk

Unit 9: Abolitionist tin of sugar

Unit 10: First-century minas from Israel

© Simon Smith 2015. Reproduced with permission from *Valuing Money* by Chris Hudson (Barnabas in Schools, 2015) www.barnabasinschools.org.uk

About the author

Chris Hudson is a member of BRF's Barnabas in Schools team. An experienced teacher, author and trainer, dedicated to promoting high-quality teaching and learning in primary schools, he provides regular INSET for schools on a variety of themes related to the Bible and Christianity, together with Barnabas RE Day storytelling, drama and music workshops for schoolchildren.

Barnabas RE Days
Exploring Christianity creatively

A Barnabas RE Day is a full day's visit to your school to bring the Bible to life for primary-aged children through a range of the creative arts, exploring themes which address many PSHE/ Citizenship objectives.

The sessions use different creative arts according to the particular skills of the team member undertaking your booking, such as storytelling, music, dance, mime, drama or creative writing. The material is based on biblical and historical accounts, personal story and shared experience. The timetable, class groupings and themes are completely flexible to suit your school's needs.

For more information, visit **www.barnabasinschools.org.uk**, email **barnabas@brf.org.uk** or contact the Barnabas Team Administrator on 01865 319704.

Other resources from Barnabas in Schools

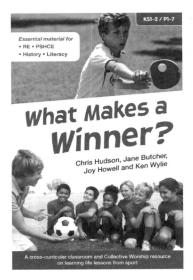

What Makes a Winner? £6.99
ISBN 978 1 84101 742 6, 96pp

What Price Peace? £8.99
ISBN 978 1 84101 691 7, 192pp

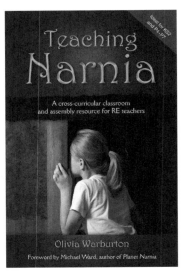

Teaching Narnia £6.99
ISBN 978 0 85746 256 5, 96pp

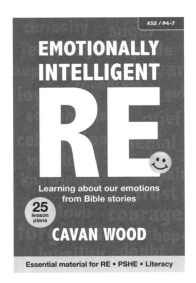

Emotionally Intelligent RE £7.99
ISBN 978 1 84101 617 7, 144pp

The RE Teacher's Survival
Guide £6.99
ISBN 978 0 85746 220 6, 96pp

RE in the Classroom with 4–5s
£7.99 978 1 84101 614 6, 64pp